CRE
LAND OF THE MINOANS

A Complete Fully Illustrated Coloured Guide
with Maps, Plans, Archaeological Sites,
Places of Interest & General Information

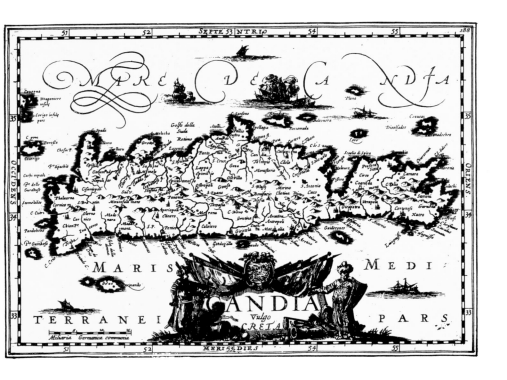

INTERWORLD
PUBLICATIONS

CRETE
LAND OF THE MINOANS

Written by
RENOS G. LAVITHIS
Historical Section
Dr. STAVROS PANTELI
Edited by
Anna Lavithis and Dr. S. Panteli

First Published in 1988
by Interworld Publications
12 The Fairway
New Barnet
Hertfordshire EN5 1HN

ISBN: 0 948853 04 2

Credit to Photographs
The bulk of the photos are taken by
  Mr. Renos Lavithis.
Other contributors are:
  Heraklis Panteris, Petros Nikolakis,
  Greek Tourist Organisation
  Sunvil Travel, S. Papadakis,
  Tom Smith, Arthur Gristwood
  Howard Lambie and others.
Also Mr. A. Nicholas who provided us with
  some excellent maps and engravings from
  his medieval collection.

Designed and produced by
  TOPHILL DESIGNS, Barnet, Herts.
Typsetting by
  Sunset Typesetters — London
Colour Planning by:
  Custance Graphics — London EC1

Printed and bound in Crete by
  G. Dedorakis Printing Works
  Industrial Center—Heraklion

INTRODUCTION —
ACKNOWLEDGEMENTS

After the great success of our Cyprus and Paphos Tourist Guides, producing a similar one for the glorious and ever friendly island of Crete was not only a top priority, but also an enormous challenge.

Visited and admired by all Europeans, Crete attracts large numbers of British and other English speaking people who, we hope, will find in this Guide most of the information which interests them.

With such a treasured island full of history, exciting scenery and golden beaches supplemented by its hospitable people and delicious food we could easily produce many volumes, therefore, we have left some room for more specialist publications.

But putting this Guide together would have been very difficult without the help of the many Cretans we met during our visits but special thanks must be given to the following:

Heraklis Panteris and his family
Stelios Koukakis and his family
Petros Nikolakakis, Socratis Argyris
the numerous Manolis's, the directors of the
Museums of Heraklion and Athens
and the Director of the Greek Tourism
Organisation in London Mr. Analytis.

CONTENTS

We will be very pleased to hear your comments and suggestions for the improvement of this publication in future editions.

4

CRETE
THROUGH THE CENTURIES
By Historian Dr. STAVROS PANTELI

Over the years Crete has been known as **"Makaronesos"** *(fortunate island),* **"Aeria"** *(airy,* owing to its fertility and unique climate), **"Doliche"** *(long,* from its shape), **"Candia"** (by the Venetians and Europeans), **"Giread"** (by the Turks), **"Collinia"** (from its numerous hills) and **"Asperia"** (from the roughness and unevenness of its soil). Crete lies almost in the centre of the eastern Mediterranean basin, southwest of the Greek mainland. Lying on Europe's southern fringe, Crete is halfway between Asia Minor and mainland Greece and is twice as far from Libya and Egypt; it also helps to enclose the Aegean Sea, a geographical factor that has had considerable influence on its history and culture. Hence, from the earliest times, Crete has served as a stepping-stone between the continents of Europe, Africa and Asia.

Crete is the 5th largest island in the Mediterranean after Sicily, Sardinia, Cyprus and Corsica and is nearly 260km long and varies in width from about 12 to 60km. Its area is about 8,280sq.km (3,200 sq. miles) and has some 1,050km of coastline. Its political and economic affairs may be domestically linked with Greece, but this beautiful island is an international archaeological and tourist attraction. Crete moreover, has survived so many challenges and incursions to its individuality that there will always be people who consider themselves first and foremost Cretans.

The history of Crete is so rich that it would take many pages to even highlight. However, the following summary should give readers a general idea of its development from the earliest years to the present day:

Palaeolithic Age
circa 8500-6500BC

It is uncertain whether or not men of the **Palaeolithic (Old Stone Age)** existed in Crete but archaeologists say that the first inhabitants of the island probably arrived around 6500BC from Asia Minor, North Africa and Anatolia and were sea farers or semi-nomadic groups. It can therefore be assumed that the earliest Neolithic (New Stone Age) culture in Crete did not develop within the island but was brought from outside. They were a Neolithic people and their stone artefacts and weapons have been found on the island along with some female figures which are thought to indicate a mother goddess cult.

Neolithic Age
Circa 6500-2600BC

The **Neolithic** *(Early, Middle and Late)* **Age,** spunned from circa, 6500 to 2600BC. Like other Neolithic people of the Mediterranean, the Cretans lived in caves or on easily defended hill-tops. In Crete however, these people seemed to have progressed at a faster rate — they developed pottery, both for domestic use and as an artform, in addition to the stone tools and weapons which they had previously used. Moreover, as the years passed they learned to build small rectangular stone (or mud-brick) houses and their burial rites appear to have changed in a manner which suggests that they abandoned, at least partially, the cult of ancestor worship.

Some of the earliest settlements were at **Knossos, Malia, Festos, Ayia Triadha, Ayia Fotia, Kamarais, Zakros** and on the **Akrotiri** peninsula near Hania.

5

Left: Marble figurine. *Right:* Gold Necklace *(Both courtesy Heraklion Museum)*

The Minoan Civilization

Around the year 3000BC copperworking was introduced; this produced a **Bronze Age** culture which is called the **MINOAN CIVILIZATION,** after the island's legendary ruler **MINOS.** Following the work at Knossos of great archaeologist Sir ARTHUR EVANS, it is now widely accepted that the Minoan Age can be divided into 3 periods, which is called **Early, Middle and Late Minoan** with each having three sub-periods. The whole period in question spuns from around 2600BC to 1050BC with the *Subminoan Age* stretching to 950BC.

During the three phases of the **EARLY MINOAN** (c2600-2300BC) some clearly marked social changes were taking place. The island's population increased rapidly; immigrants came to **Palaikastro, Mohlos** and **Gournia** from Asia Minor and the Cyclades and in the Messara there is evidence of new arrivals from Libya and Egypt who settled in many places in the plain. For the first time the population began to leave the open country and to concentrate in villages and towns and the purely pastoral society declined. Instead of each family making what it needed in wood, pottery and metal, the crafts became specialised; men whom Homer called **"Demiourgoi"** *(Creators)* set up as specialists and professionalism in craft and art was born. Moreover, the architecture of private houses, also advanced greatly.

By about 2000BC **"Palaces"** began to be built on the sites of **Knossos, Ayia Triada, Festos** and **Malia,** inaugurating the MIDDLE MINOAN (to c1600BC) or *Protopalatial Period.* Economic, political and social organizations began to flourish, with increased trade in the eastern Mediterranean while stone carving, gold work, jewellery and pottery demonstrated aesthetic progress.

Around the year 1700BC one of Crete's periodic earthquakes destroyed parts of the three major palaces but there was no break in the continuity of Minoan culture. The palaces were reconstructed and even enlarged introducing the *Middle Minoan III* or *New Palace (Neopalatical) Period.* These ambitious complexes, with a medley of sculptures, frescoes, paintings, pottery and metalwork are still visible today. Meanwhile, Cretan ships traded with countries as far as Spain — the economic advantages were massive. However by about 1500BC **Mycenaean Greeks** had assured an influential, perhaps dominant role in Minoan affairs.

Then about 1450BC a great catastrophe befell the island-cities and villages were destroyed by the severe eruption of the volcano of THIRA *(Santorini, the ancient Kallisti)* north of Crete. Most of the old sites were reoccupied but the next 400 years were marked by the steady decadence of the splendid Minoan civilisation. Eventually the **Dorians**, another Greek-speaking people, moved in and organized Crete, while some Minoans retreated into the mountains, to become known later as **ETEOCRETANS** *("True Cretans.")*

Without a shadow of doubt the MINOANS *(a short race, with the men averaging just a little over 5 feet)*, were far ahead of their time in many aspects of their life and they set the stage of much of what was to follow in the Eastern Mediterranean. The Minoan remains in Crete continue and will continue to fascinate all visitors.

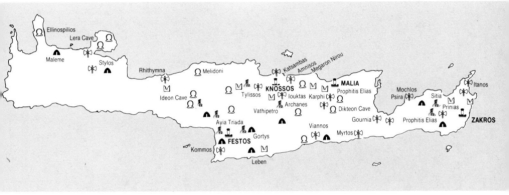

MAP OF MINOAN CRETE

 Minoan Palaces   Ancient Settlements

M   Sacred Peaks   Estates & Villas

Ω   Sacred Caves   Tholos Tombs

Geometric/ Hellenistic & other Periods

Even though Minoan civilisation was supplanted eventually, Crete still played a part in the transfer of various cultural forms from the Near East to Greece. Before the Roman conquest of 67BC, Crete went through the so called **Protogeometric: 950-800BC, Geometric: 800-700BC, Dedalic: 700-550BC** and **Hellenistic 550-67BC** Periods. Though there is no more elaborate palace architecture, building techniques survived, as we know from the evidence of tombs, and there were fresh innovations in pottery. However, in those troubled times of transition, some of the native population took to the mountains and built settlements of refuge for themselves in high places such as **Karphi** *(the nail)*, **Kavousi** and **Vrokastro**. Nevertheless the increasing use of iron by the beginning of the 10th century contributed to the formation of smaller separate city-state communities which contrast with the centralised uniformity of Late Minoan times. Similarly the growth of iron-working led to the closer attachment of domestic industry to agriculture, resulting in an increased self-sufficiency of village producers independent of markets.

By the beginning of the 8th century BC conditions in Crete had become more settled and a few old Minoan sites like **Ayia Triadha,**

7

Festos and **Malia** were once again inhabited. Gradually the refuge settlements of the troubled period of transition were abandoned or were developed into city-states. Thus in the following two centuries a significant increase of prosperity and of population is apparent, with the foundation of new cities and the expansion of older ones.

LAW CODES OF GORTYS

Before we proceed with a brief study of the Roman period we must mention the world-famous **Law Code of Gortys** — the earliest written legal document in Europe. It must be pointed out that the cities of Crete played a great part in the development and codification of civil laws and the Cretans were much admired as authorities in the field of juris prudence and political philosophy throughout classical times.

Though the **Gortys Code** was inscribed in the first half of the 5th century BC *(probably around 450BC)*, it incorporates even older material in the sense that various statues amend prior written law — and modify even earlier customs — relevant to various topics.

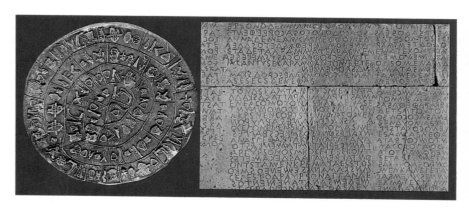

Above: The Festos Disk 17th cent. BC, now at Heraklion Museum.
Above right: Part of the ancient Law Code of Gortys.
(Courtesy Heraklion Museum)

The first inscribed stone of the Laws to be found was discovered in 1857 in the wall of a water-mill near the ruined church of *St. Titus* at Gortys. The inscription is written in 12 columns, each originally five blocks high, of which four now remain. Each column is about 1½ metres (five feet) high and there are 53 to 56 lines of writing, the height of the letters being about 2.5cm (one inch).

The document is of inestimable value and is the chief source of our knowledge of the social history of Crete in the early historical period. The text consists of a series of laws relating to citizenship, marriage, tenure of property and inheritance etc. Each pronouncement is in the form *"If such and such happens, then the legal position is that . . ."*

Lightly called the "Queen of Inscriptions" the Gortys Law Code is certainly a mine of information about the lives and habits of the people who lived in one of the chief city states of ancient Crete. Archaeological research has certainly paid rich dividends and has made the work of historians so much simpler.

The Romans

The next rulers of Crete were the **ROMANS** who occupied the island from **67BC-395AD** i.e. for 462 years. Following a war which lasted for around 2½ years, Q. Caecillus Metellus eventually subdued Crete. This earned him the title *"Creticus"*. It is believed however, that the resistance offered by the Cretans was so determined that the island was almost depopulated before it could be conquered. It appears that the island first became a Roman province but later joined with Cyrenaica for administrative purposes although we know that the two provinces were separate in 44BC. Augustus (27BC-AD14) however subsequently joined its two dependancies and made them into one senatorial province under a governor of Praetorian rank. This arrangement lasted until the reign of Diocletian (284-305AD) when Crete again became a separate province.

In the decades that followed the conquest, Crete was settled by groups of veterans who found excellent land for cultivation and were the first centres from which spread the influence of Rome. Among other privileges that were granted, the triumvir Antony, seeking allies in his war with Caesar's killers *(Julius Caesar was murdered on 13 March 44BC)*, had granted financial exemptions to the cities and had conferred Roman citizenship on some of the inhabitants. As a result Crete (owing to its position on the main Roman trade routes between East and West), enjoyed the advantages of material prosperity and of internal peace, which had been destroyed in the past by continual internal struggles. Thus, the distribution of the population remained unchanged under Rome. The government assisted the development of agriculture, both by securing peace and by improving the land and by works of engineering; and for political and other reasons some cities (e.g. *Knossos and Gortys)* were especially favoured, while others, which had flourished previously suffered a decline. **Gortys,** the Roman capital of Crete, had probably around fifty thousand inhabitants and the great geographer Strabo says that the city measured 50 stadia i.e. 9.5 kilometres across.

Archaeological remains confirm that Crete seems to have remained secluded, self contained, enjoying the material prosperity which resulted from Roman rule, but without any renewal of energy and life, clinging to the old traditions. It must also be noted that Christianity, traditionally introduced by **St. Paul,** who was driven ashore on Crete in 47AD gathered momentum under the Apostle's appointee, **Bishop Titus.**

Early Byzantine Period

After the Roman Empire was divided, Crete passed to **Byzantium (the Eastern Roman Empire) in 395AD.** This first **Byzantium period lasted to 824AD.** A notable event were the Arab raids of 651. The peace enjoyed by Crete was disturbed when the Arabs overrun the island. The Arabs maintained a base for piracy in Crete until 674 when they abandoned it.

In 823AD, civil war at the heart of the Empire provided the Arabs with an opportunity to seize the outlying islands of Sicily and Crete. In the same year Saracen Arabs from Spain led by Emir Abu Hafs Umar b. Isa plundered the island. In 824 they returned with the same Emir and around forty ships and landed a large force near where Heraklion now stands. The Emir it has been recorded, burnt his ships to ensure that his men have no thought of abandoning Crete — *"flowing"*, as he said *"with milk and honey"*. They set up a fortress surrounded by a deep trench at a spot indicated to them, according to tradition, by a hermit. They were soon the masters of the whole island. They called their capital **"Hadak";** it was known to the Byzantines as **"Handax"** and to the Venetians and Turks as **"Candia"** before it acquired its modern name of **Heraklion.**

9

Arabic Occupation

The **Arabic Occupation** lasted from **824-961AD**. For 137 years Heraklion was a stronghold from which Arab pirates from Spain, Africa and Egypt ravaged the coasts and islands of Greece. A slave market was held there which supplied the *Emirs* of the east with the flower of Greek youth and beauty to adorn their courts and fill their harems. The Metropolitan **Cyril** was martyred when the Roman capital Gortys fell to the Arabs and his cathedral, the church of St. Titus was destroyed. In all nineteen cities are said to have been sacked and only in the mountains *(in places like Sphakia to the southwest of the island)* did a handful of Christians survive.

This period therefore *(from 824-961AD)*, witnessed a massive depopulation and economic ruin of the island. However, from 825-950AD, five major expenditionary forces were sent by the Byzantine Emperors to recover Crete from the Saracens. All failed because of the incompetence of the leaders. In 960, however, the island fell to **Nicephoros Phokas**. The Saracen stronghold of Heraklion fell on 7 March 961.

Second Byzantine Period

The **Second Byzantine Period** *(Eastern Roman Empire)*, lasted from **961 to 1204**. The island was ruled by a *Duke of Crete* who was its civil governor and supreme military commander. The Duke and his staff were in the main chosen from the kin of the Emperor. A kind of feudalism seems to have been introduced at this time by the noble families who lived in Crete and by those who settled there. The lands belonging to these families were cultivated by a class of men called *"Parici"* who were Christianised Arabs, and by Serfs who were prisoners of war or simply bought slaves.

Heraklion became the civil and religious capital of the island. Furthermore, the Patriarchate of Constantinople restored the church in Crete and retained the names of the bishoprics as they had been before the Arab occupation, although the former metropolitan cities had disappeared. Gortys, Knossos, Arkadia, Ierapetra, Hersonissos, Kydonia, Syvritos, Lappa and Kissamos, were no more, but their bishops lived and worked in other places which often came to be called **"Episkopi"**. The metropolitan of Gortys became Archbishop of Crete and removed to Heraklion where a cathedral was built and dedicated, like that of Gortys to the Apostle Titus, the patron Saint of Crete.

On the whole, the history of Crete from 961 to 1204 was relatively uneventful, except for the seizure of the island by the rebel admiral **Caryses** in 1092. The Cretans took the side of the imperial forces and killed Caryses. It must be noted that the island's population showed a marked upsurge, reaching probably 250,000 in 1204.

By 1200AD the Empire, ruled from Constantinople had so shrunk that there remained only Asia Minor, Thrace, Eastern and Central Macedonia, Thessaly, Crete and a few other islands.

Christ's disciples and the Virgin among them observe the Christ Pantocrator blessing them (not in the picture). A wall painting from Panayia Kera *(see page 125)*

Venetian Expansion Fourth Crusade)

The story of the acquisition of Crete by Venice is contained in the involved politics of the **Fourth Crusade,** proclaimed by Pope Innocent in 1202. Predominantly a French enterprise the Fourth Crusade, diverted by Venetian cunning first to Zara, a Christian city on the Dalmatian coast and then onto Constantinople *(for 900 years this great christian city commanded the trade routes between Asia, Russia and Europe and was the bastion and guardian of civilisation)* ostensibly in order to restore to the throne the deposed Angeli rulers, captured it in 1204 and then set about sharing out among themselves the remnants of the Byzantine Empire. It was Constantinople's darkest hour — perhaps even darker than that of 1453 which saw the city's final fall to the Ottoman Sultan. The action of the Crusaders was beyond doubt one of the most despicable acts in history.

Lord Norwich in his masterly study **"A History of Venice"** wrote as follows:

"There are few greater ironies in history than the fact that the fate of Eastern Christianity should have been sealed — and half of Europe condemned to some 500 years of Muslim rule — by men who fought under the banner of the Cross. Those men were transported, inspired, encouraged and ultimately led by *Enrico Dandolo* in the name of the Venetian Republic; and, just as Venice derived the major advantage from the tragedy, so she and her magnificent old **Doge** *(Chief Magistrate, in fact lender)*, must accept the major responsibility for the havoc they wrought upon the world."

Of all the Levantine possessions acquired by Venice, as a result of the Fourth Crusade, by far the most important was the great island of Crete, which she obtained on 12 August 1204, from Boniface of Montferrat to whom it had been given 15 months earlier by Alexios IV, at the cost of 1,000 marks of silver. Boniface signed the famous document of cession, the *Refutatio Cretae,* and this became the legal root of title by which Venice held the island.

Venetian Rule

The **Venetian Occupation** lasted from **1204 to 1669** — in all 465 years. However, even before the Venetians *(were engaged elsewhere)* had time to take possession of the island, their great rivals, the **GENOESE,** had established a colony there. Around the year 1206, *Errico Pescatori,* the Genoese pirate and self-styled Count of Malta, landed an army on the island and occupied Heraklion where a Genoese fifth column had already been organised. He met no resistance in the countryside and consolidated his position by building 14 or 15 forts *(castelli)* in readiness for a Venetian invasion. The Venetians triumphed in the end but it was not till the armistice with Genoa in 1212 that the first comprehensive attempt at colonisation was made and the organisation of a Cretan government was undertaken. Under the Venetians, the society of Crete had a strictly feudal structure. The highest civil and military power was in the hands of the **Duke,** who was a Venetian nobleman elected by the Venetian Assembly for a period of two years. After the Duke, came the two **Counsellors** *(Consiliarii),* who were elected in the same manner for two years.

The island was soon divided into **fiefs** *(feudal estates)* and this was strongly resented by the natives. In fact what distinguishes the medieval history of Crete from that of the other conquered possessions in the Near East is the almost constant insubordination of the Cretan population. One insurrection followed another in rapid succession, and the first 160 years of Venetian rule are little else than a record of risings. Those led by the **Hagiostephanitais** in 1212 and by **Alexios Kallerges** in 1283-1299 were extremely serious. Other revolts took place in 1217-19, 1230-36, 1261 and 1364-66.

11

MARE

DEL

ARCIPE

LAGO

MARE

MEDITER

RANEO

CANDIA uel Creta insula
posta nel mare Mediterraneo
locho delli Ill.mi S.i Veneciani
piena di degne antiquitadi,
et insula fertile di ogni gusta,
et principalmente di unico ui-
no, quala di longezza tiene da
mill. 260. di largezza mill 50.
et di circuito mill. 520. Et dis-
tante dal capo di Otranto
mill: 500. di Alessandria mill 450.
Delle Soria mill. 660. Di Aff-
rice mill: 250.

48

12

In short, the Venetian power structure, made little acknowledgement of the already existing Cretan ruling class. Old established estates were confiscated, rights and customs were swept away, and the Venetians attacked the Cretan religion. The Greek Orthodox Archbishop and bishops were driven away and their cathedrals were handed over to Latin prelates appointed by the Pope. Monks and priests were allowed to remain but were subjected to financial pressure and to other forms of discrimination. All Cretans *(local nobility, priests and common people)*, therefore united in their unrelenting struggle against their Venetian oppressors. Thus native Cretans never abandoned the Orthodox religion, the Greek language and their popular lore, although the long and relentless oppression on them by the Venetians led to a high emigration rate.

With the fall of Constantinople on Tuesday 29 May 1453, the menace of Ottoman domination of south eastern Europe, the Mediterranean region and the Middle East, loomed nearer and nearer. Turkish pirates in 1471 destroyed 14 villages in Sitia and in 1498 the monastery of Our Lady of the Headland at Toplou was pillaged. In 1567, the Turks took Sudha in a night attack, sacking and burning the town. By 1571, Venice had lost to Turkey all her possessions in Greece and also Cyprus. Crete however was defended for almost another century, until 1669.

As a result of the so-called Great War of 1645-1669, between Venice and the Ottoman Empire, Crete was lost. On 1 May 1648, the Turks already possessing parts of Crete, began attempts to capture Heraklion. The city was to hold out alone for 21 years; the formal *"great siege"* of the city began in May 1667 and ended on 5 September 1669. The cost of the siege, one of the longest in history, (Byron called it *"Troy's rival"*), had been enormous. The Venetians, it was calculated had lost 30,985 men and the Turks 118,754 and the Republic had spent 4,253.000 ducats upon the defence of this one city. The native population was also drastically reduced.

Turkish Occupation

The **Turkish Occupation** lasted from **1669 to 1898**. The Turks did nothing to develop or even to maintain the economic life of the island. They collected the poll-tax on every Christian and Jew and made a levy of up to $\frac{1}{7}$ on all agricultural produce but the infrastructure on which high productivity depended was almost completely neglected. Whereas the Venetians made roads, bridges and aqueducts, the Turks created nothing and moreover, allowed the former means of communications to decay. Religious persecution was on the whole spasmodic in character and tended to be directed more against the higher echelons of the clergy than against the laity.

During the next 150 years large-scale disturbances only occured in Crete when external events encouraged the Cretans to think that they could obtain outside assistance towards their goal of freedom. Thus in 1692 **Domenigo Mocenigo** the Venetian Captain-General gave naval support to a force of around 2,000 Cretans who attacked Hania. It was unsuccessful. In 1770 after the Cretan leader **Daskaloyiannis** obtained a promise of help from the Russians *(whose fleet was roaming the Mediterranean Sea)* he raised a force of 800 men and held the Turks at Hania. The Russians however, defeated the Turkish fleet off Chios but did nothing else to help the Cretans. Daskaloyiannis was soon executed.

In the early years of the 19th century, a great movement for independence grew up in Greece. Initially it concentrated on the mainland and in the Ionian Islands but its success encouraged two localised Cretan revolts. The first of these took place in the summer of 1821 when the men of **Sfakia** rose up in arms to avenge the massacre of 30 Christians at Hania and the murder of the Metropolitan and five bishops at the Cathedral altar in Heraklion By the Spring of 1824 the rising was over — partly crushed by the Egyptian troops summoned by the Sultan to help. The second wa incited by the natives of the island of **Grabousa** *(following the defea of Turkey at the naval battle of Navarino on 27 October 1827),* whe sent one of their leaders *(the Epirot called Hadjimichalis)* into Crete t stir up a revolt. He was soon defeated by the Turks a **Frangokastello** in 1828; he was captured and cut into small pieces

Between 1822, when the Egyptian troops were first summoned to Crete and 1840, the island was governed on behalf of the Sultan by the *Viceroy of Egypt.* In 1830 Egyptian rule received the official sanction of the Great Powers (Britain, France, Italy and Russia) who had taken Crete nominally under their protection. Egyptian rule was opportunistic and oppressive. This rule fell even more heavily upon the Moslems than upon the Christians, the result being that the population of the island which in 1821 numbered 289,000 had shrunk by 1840 to 129,000.

In 1840 Crete once more passed under Turkish control and in 184 both Christians and Moslems tried to exploit the situation and improve their lot. Whereas the Moslems were content to reques reduction in taxation and administrative reforms, many of the Christian leaders demanded union with Greece. Encouraged by the Cretan Committee which had been set up in Athens, the Cretans o the Region of **Sfakia** *(Sfakiots)* revolted. Yet, although these Sfakiots rose in strength, they were unable to stand up to vastly superior forces. For the next 15 years Crete remained quiet, during which time the Albanian governor ruling on behalf of the Sultan showed more severity towards the Turkish beys than towards the Christians. Faced with heavy exactions, many of the Moslems sol their estates and left the island. As a consequence more and more land passed into Christian hands — a development which had already begun at the time of the Egyptian occupation. What is more the Christian population of Crete steadily increased. The next majo revolt had begun in 1866 and lasted until 1868; this again was only suppressed with the aid of Egyptian troops.

The heroic defence of the monastery of ARKADI is long remembered by all Cretans with pride and gratitude and is commemorated at an annual festival on 10 November. After two days intense fighting, the brave defenders, like those of Mesolonghi some 40 years before, blew up their powder magazines. On this occasion 450 Turks perished along with over 400 Greeks. Arkadi has been, ever since, the symbol of the island's motto *"Freedom or Death".* Also remembered with much reverance was the blockade — running activities of SS Arkadi in which the Englishman J.E. Hilary Skinner travelled to Crete from Syria in March 1867. SS Arkadi penetrated the Turkish blockade more than 20 times.

After 1868 the Sultan promalgated a series of reforms embodied i what is known as the Organic Statute. This however satisfied neithe the Cretans nor the ruling class of Turks in Crete and in 1876 th islanders presented fresh demands. Eventually, the *Pact of Halep* was signed in 1878 in the house of the Mitsotakis family (at a subur of Hania) who had played a significant part in the negotiations Today it is regarded by many Cretans as the first step on the road t freedom and to unity with Greece.

In 1889 the Pact of Halepa was annulled by the Sultan and in th early months of 1896 civil war erupted in Hania between th

Christians and the Moslems. Under pressure from the European Powers, the Sultan agreed amongst other things to call a National Assembly of Cretans, to renew the Pact of Halepa, appoint a Christian governor and proclaim a general amnesty. On 4 September 1896 the new Governor, **George Betovic,** a former Prince of Samos, took office but his authority lasted little more than five months and war between the Christians and Moslems again broke out at Hania in February 1897. The Christians once again proclaimed union with Greece and this time received prompt aid. On 10 February **Prince George,** the second son of King George I of Greece, led a flotilla of topedo-boats to intercept Turkish reinforcements and on 15 February a Greek army commanded by **Colonel Vassos** *(the King's aide-de-camp)*, landed west of Hania. The admirals of the European Powers (Britain, France, Italy, Russia, Germany and Austria-Hungary), whose flagships were at Suda Bay, sent an International landing party on 15 February and finally put an end to the fighting by separating the combatants. They then occupied Hania and by that act ended for ever all but the shadow of Turkish rule in Crete.

Cretan Autonomy and Union with Greece

The Turks were finally ejected in 1898 and the island was granted autonomous status under a High Commissioner. **Prince George** accepted the office and landed at Suda on 21 December 1898. But nothing short of Union with Greece would satisfy many Cretans. Among them was the Cretan bom **Eleftherios Venizelos** *(the "saviour and founder of modern Greece")*. In 1905 the Cretan leaders withdrew from the Chamber of Deputies and from the Assembly and united under Venizelos. They set up headquarters in a house high in the White Mountains, above the village of *Therissos* from which they proclaimed the **Freedom of Crete and its Union with Greece.** Today Venizelo's House has become a place of pilgrimage for Cretan patriots.

Eventually, and leaving all details aside, Greece and Turkey signed a treaty on 14 November 1913 in which a common frontier was delineated and Crete definitely assigned to Greece. The island was formally taken over on **14 December 1913** by King Constantine, at whose side were the Crown Prince George *(who never became king)* and Venizelos, the Prime Minister.

British troops stationed in Crete under the Great Powers protection treaty parade at Candia during the Kings Birthday *(H. Panteris Collection)*

Freedom Fighters with their leader at Therisso—1905. *(H. Panteris Collection)*

The Battle of Crete

Since then Crete has shared most of Greece's history. On 28 October 1940 the Greek government rejected an ultimatum by the Italians whose army already confronted them from the Albanian frontier. This was the famous **OXI (No)** which resounds through Greek history and is commemorated each year by a public holiday. The Italians were repulsed but their more powerful allies, the Germans succeeded. In 1941, the Greek government along with British, Commonwealth and Greek troops were forced by the advancing Germans to retreat from mainland Greece to Crete. Shortly thereafter, on 20 May the Germans launched probably history's first, purely **airborne invasion,** putting down all organised resistance within 10 days. Most of the Allied forces were eventually evacuated from the southern coast but the Cretans were left to another occupation till the last German troops surrendered in May 1945.

Modern Crete

Post war Crete made a slow recovery but since the 1950's it has benefitted from growing international commerce and tourism especially since the late 1970's.

Finally, it must be stressed that throughout the long centuries of resistance against foreign rulers many Cretans — like **Captain Michalis** in *Kazantzaki's* novel **"Freedom and Death** — were driven to fight by their passionate belief in a free Crete. At times however, the majority were fighting not for an ideal but out of necessity to safeguard their families, their homes, their villages and their land. As pointed out above, many Cretans in earlier centuries were protected by the relative isolation of their mountain villages. Later, and again partly because of their remoteness, some of these villages became famous centres of rebellion and were often the target of severe reprisals by the occupying power. **Anoyia,** for example, has been twice destroyed in the last 170 years — once by fire in 1822 on the orders of the occupying power and again on 15 August 1944 when the Germans systematically destroyed the entire village. The case of Anoyia, although dramatic, is not exceptional; numerous villages have suffered both from reprisals and from conventional war damage.

HANIA TOWN

Together with Heraklion, Hania acts as the administrative centre of Greece in Crete. It is a very pleasant town dominated by the Venetian harbour and the old Venetian quarter which is well preserved.

The siege of Hania by the Turks.

17

HISTORY

Hania is built over the ancient city of **KYDONIA** which was the centre of the **KYDONIAS,** early pre-Greek people who were ruled by *King Kydon,* son of Apollo. Finds in the Kastelli quarter (see below), revealed that the city has been inhabited since the Neolithic period and that civilisation continued throughout the centuries. The Minoans were here, so were the Romans who established a large city with a theatre.

During the early Christian period it was a See of a Bishop. Unfortunately it was destroyed by the Arabs when they took over the island and the city lost its importance.

After the Venetian occupation in 1252, Hania recovered considerably and was called **LA CANEA.** Venetian rule lasted until 1645 except for a very brief period when it was occupied by the Genoese in the 13th century. As LA CANEA was the closest port of Crete to Venice, it soon became an important centre and many fine buildings, private and public were erected. It became known as **"The Venice of the East".**

In the latter years, in anticipation of a Turkish invasion the defences were strengthened with new walls, bastions and a great moat. However, after a siege of two months Hania fell into Turkish hands in 1645. It then became the administrative capital of the island, the Pasha's *Seraghio* was established and a large community of Arabs and Africans settled.

In 1898 the Turks were finally ejected from Crete when the Great Powers took over the administration and Prince George became a High Commissioner — *see history section.*

Above: An old engraving of Hania Lighthouse
(H. Panteris Collection)
Below: The entrance to the harbour. To the right is the lighthouse and to the left is Firkas and the northern city walls.

MUSEUMS AT HANIA

(1) THE ARCHAEOLOGICAL MUSEUM

It is housed inside the Venetian church of ST. FRANCIS. The interior of the building is of great architectural interest and the small but well presented collection of finds, mainly from Western Crete, includes vases, terracottas, sealstones, fine mosaics, glassware, jewellery, coins, armaments and sculptures. In the side court there is a fine Turkish fountain and old fragments of buildings.
25 Halydon Street, Tel. 24418.

(2) THE HISTORICAL MUSEUM

It houses a fine collection of archives from all over Crete and other parts of Greece including many rare documents covering the Byzantine, Venetian and Turkish periods; also from modern Crete. There are also exhibits connected with the Cretan's struggle for freedom including flags, armaments and photographs covering the Battle of Crete and the German occupation.
1 Sfakianaki Street, Tel. 22606.

(3) THE NAVAL MUSEUM

This is situated on the Western side of the harbour within the city walls. A small, but interesting collection, associated with the marine history of Crete.

During the summer there are performances of Cretan dancing, singing and drama within the castle, by the Museum.
Akti Koundourioti, Tel. 26437

The Interior of the Archaeological Museum housing a very interesting collection.

WHAT TO SEE IN HANIA CITY

Hania is really two cities, the old walled city with its medieval quarters and the new city with the suburbs spreading around the old.

THE NEW CITY

(4) PUBLIC MARKET: Built in a cruciform shape in 1911, the market is unique in Crete and is modelled on the great Market of Marseilles. Here you can get all kinds of foodstuffs, ranging from cheeses, nuts, drinks, fish, fruit and vegetables.

(5) PUBLIC GARDENS: These lovely gardens were laid out in 1870 by a Turkish Pasha. They provide an ideal place to relax. There is a bandstand in the centre, a cafeteria, playground for children and a small zoo.

To the east of the city is KHALEPA quarter where all the European representatives and merchants were staying at the turn of the century. Here too was the "Palace" of Prince George and the House of Eleftherios Venizelos. His statue is standing outside.

In this quarter, there are two churches, a modern and large church for the community and *St. Mary Magdalene* of Russian style dating to 1909.

THE OLD CITY

It was surrounded with walls of which only parts survived. The city provides most of the souvenir shops where you can have a wonderful time shopping and some parts retain their old Venetian character with the narrow streets and old buildings.

The WALLS had a total perimeter of 3km and there was a moat 50 metres wide and 10 metres deep. The best preserved bastions are SCHIAVO, LANDO and SAN DIMITRIO.

The old city of Hania is divided into five quarters.

KASTELLI QUARTER — The original site of the Neolithic town, the Minoan city and the kingdom of KYDON. Due to its high ground position it was expanded by the Venetians. It suffered extensive damage during the second world war.

19

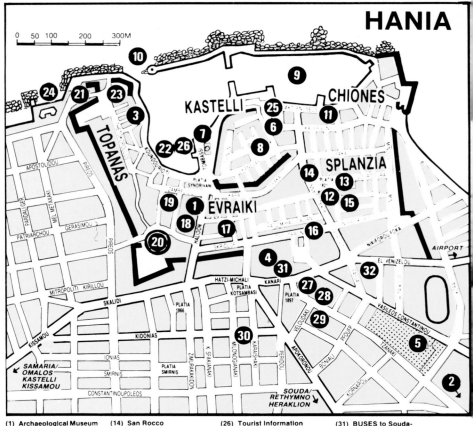

HANIA

KASTELLI CHIONES

TOPANAS

APOSTOLIDOU

SPLANZIA

EVRAIKI

AIRPORT →

(1) Archaeological Museum
(2) Historical Museum
(3) Naval Museum
(4) Public Market
(5) Public Gardens & Zoo
(6) Arcade of St. Mark
(7) Djamassi Mosque
(8) Minoan Kidonia
(9) Venetian Harbour
(10) Lighthouse
(11) Venetian Arsenali
(12) 1821 Square
(13) St. Nicholas Church

(14) San Rocco
(15) Ayii Anargyri Church
(16) Minaret
(17) Orthodox Cathedral
(18) Roman Catholic Church
(19) Venetian Loggia
(20) Shiave Bastion
(21) Revieri Gate
(22) Koundouriotis
     Promenade
(23) San Salvator Church
(24) Swimming Pool
(25) Customs

(26) Tourist Information
     Office
(27) Post Office
(28) O.T.E. (Telephones)
(29) Olympic Airways
(30) Tourist Police

(31) BUSES to Souda-
     Rethymno-Heraklion-
     Akrotiri-Chora-Sfakion-
     Also town routes
(32) BUSES to Akrotiri-
     Rethymno-Heraklion

(6) ARCADE OF ST. MARK — It was once the "Corso" (the place where people on foot promenade up and down) of the Venetian rulers.

(7) MOSQUE OF DIAMISSI or as also known, *"Mosque of Hassan Pasha"*. It was built in 1645 and the original domes survive. Now it houses the Tourist Information Office and has a small exhibition of local handicrafts.

(8) MINOAN KYDONIA — Some remains of the old civilization, situated by Kanevaro Street.

CHIONES QUARTER — Situated to the east of Kastelli.

(9) THE VENETIAN HARBOUR, well protected by a breakwater to the north, it had shipbuilding and repairing workshops and warehouses.

(10) THE LIGHTHOUSE is situated at the end of the breakwater and close to the north eastern side of TOPANAS QUARTER. You can walk all along to the lighthouse from where you get excellent views of the town. The tower is modern, 19th century.

(11) ARSENALI. The original shipbuilding and repairs dockyards, dating to the 15th and 17th centuries. Parts of the buildings still survive.

SPLANZIA QUARTER to the south of Chiones.

(12) 1821 SQUARE — The large plane tree dominating the square is a monument as it was used by the Turks to hang the Greek Orthodox bishop in 1821.

(13) CHURCH OF ST. NICHOLAS —It was originally a Dominican Monastery, converted into the Imperial Mosque of Sultan Ibrahim and in 1912 it became an Orthodox Church. You cannot miss the bell tower and the minaret.

(14) SAN ROCCO — Venetian church, by the side of 1821 Square, with some inscriptions dating to 1630. It is at present closed.

Above: The large cruciform shaped Public Market. *Below right:* A fruit shop inside the Market.
Below left: An old Venetian style street.

(15) AYII ANARGYRI — An orthodox church, one of very few which was allowed to function under both the Venetians and the Turks. It contains excellent old icons and was dedicated to Kosmas and Damianos.

(16) MINARET — The remains of a mosque, mainly the Minaret, in Hadzimikhali Daliani Street.

EVRAÏKI (Jewish) QUARTER —

The area around the south part of the promenade with numerous cafes, tavernas and souvenir shops. It is dominated by the VENIZELOS SQUARE known also as *SANTRIVANI SQUARE*.

(1) CHURCH OF ST. FRANCIS *(Also see Museum)*. One of the finest of the surviving Venetian buildings in Crete, it has a strong Gothic influence, now preserved as the Archaeological Museum.

(17) ORTHODOX CATHEDRAL — Is called, *the church of TRIMARTYRI-* "Three Martyrs" of 1860's. It was built by a Turk whose son was believed to have been saved by Virgin Mary's miracle.

TOPANAS QUARTER — The most cosmopolitan quarter. Situated to the west of the harbour, the quarter has some of the finest Venetian streets and houses.

(21) REVIERI GATE with the **escutcheon** (a shield on which a coat of arms is shown) of the Revieri family inscribed in 1608. Through the gate there is a Venetian chapel and nearby to the left are Venetian buildings, powder magazines and armoury stores.

(3) FIRKAS — The northern walls and bastions incorporating the Naval Museum. It was here that the Greek flag was officially hoisted in 1913 Uniting Crete with Greece.

(22) AKTI KOUNDOURIOTIS — a picturesque promenade lined with cafes, tavernas and souvenir shops. An ideal place for an evening stroll or to sip ouzo in the taverna and watch the world go by.

(23) SAN SALVATOR BASTION — Here, behind the Bastion is the aband Venetian church of San Salvator.

General view of the Venetian Harbour with the Arsenali in the background.

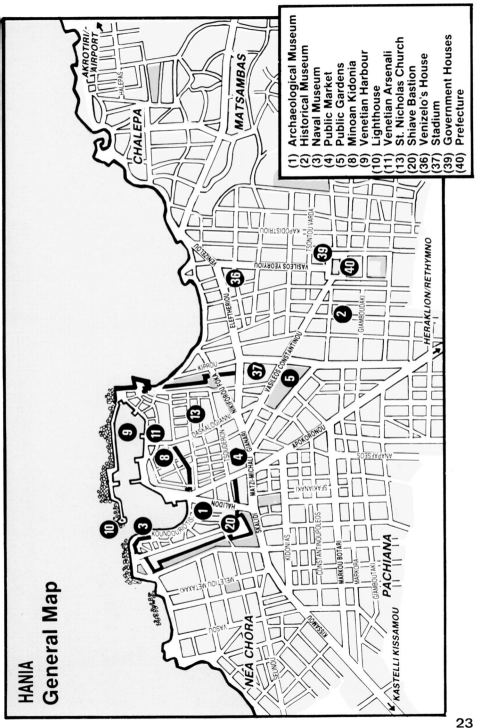

HANIA
General Map

(1) Archaeological Museum
(2) Historical Museum
(3) Naval Museum
(4) Public Market
(5) Public Gardens
(8) Minoan Kidonia
(9) Venetian Harbour
(10) Lighthouse
(11) Venetian Arsenali
(13) St. Nicholas Church
(20) Shiave Bastion
(36) Venizelo's House
(37) Stadium
(39) Government Houses
(40) Prefecture

ENTERTAINMENT

Hania is a cosmopolitan city well known for its delicious cuisine and its many good restaurants and tavernas, some in excellent spots.

There are also a number of good music spots mainly bouzouki places and Cretan music clubs. Most of the night spots are outside of the town and operate mainly during the summer months and include ZAMANIA on the road to Souda, PANGRITIO near Souda, MOURNIANO KONAKI at Mournia village etc.

There are numerous discotheques both at Hania and Souda catering for the young.

The Munincipal Theatre has its centre at the FIRKAS Bastion where it performs with drama, music dance etc.

PUBLIC TRANSPORT —
Local Services to and around Hania.
BUS — 1 *to:* Halepa-Akrotiri-Airport
BUS — 2 *to:* Souda Bay-Souda Harbour
BUS — 3 *to:* Galatas-Filakes Ayias
BUS — 4 *to:* Mournies-Korakes
KTEL 27119

USEFUL ADDRESSES
Tel. Code (0821)
TOURIST INFORMATION OFFICE (EOT)
Akti Tombasi-Harbour .... Tel: 26426
TOURIST POLICE — 44 Karaiskaki St. 24477
HOSPITAL 27231
FIRST AID 22550
HARBOUR POLICE — 21 Akti Tombasi 22600
Souda Police — Souda Harbour 89316
Customs — Katehaki Square 89240

OLYMPIC AIRWAYS—84 Tzanakaki St... 27701/3
ANEK Steamship Company, S. Venizelos St. 23636
　　　　　　　　　　　　　　　　　　　51915
POST OFFICE — Tzanakaki St. 24609
Telephones & Telegrams (OTE)
　Tzanakaki St. 52499
Archaeological Museum — Chalidon St. 24418
Public Library — 6-8 Dragouni St. 27231/5
ELPA (Greek Automobile Association)
　Veronitis Passa St. 26059
Emergencies 100
Consulates
French Consulate, 12 El. Venizelos St. 23102
German Consulate, Platia (Square) Agoras 28712
Swedish Consulate, Tzanakaki St. 28712
Sports
Swimming Pool — Akti Kanari 24387
Sailing Club — Demokratias Ave. 21293/4
Tennis Club — Demokratias Ave. 24010
Nautical Club 24384
Hunting Club 24751
Mountain Climbing
KALERGI PEAK — Height 1680 metres —
　40 places 24646
VOLIKAS PEAK — Height 1480 metres —
　30 places 24647
Banks: Bank of Crete 53745
　　　Bank of Greece 22768
　　　National Bank 22413
　　　Commercial Bank 23031
　　　Credit Bank 27703
　　　Ionian & Popular 22508

A view of the Topanas and Akti Kountourioti.

ARCHAEOLOGICAL SITES

Not many ancient Minoan sites have been discovered in the western side of the island. Most of the ancient cities cover the post Minoan, Archaic, Hellenistic and Roman periods; below we state the regions most important sites.

APTERA *(Featherless)*, one of the largest ancient cities of Crete, it derived its name from a contest between MUSES and SIRENES at the *Museion* (spot of the city). The MUSES won with their charm and music, the defeated SIRENES plucked off their feathers and cast themselves into the sea. The ancient city is situated by the southern entrance to Souda Bay and was an important centre between 5th century BC and 4th century AD. Remains to be seen include Cyclopean Walls, a Hellenistic Temple dedicated to Demeter, Dorian Bass reliefs and inscriptions, and underground Roman cisterns.

PHALASARNA — An ancient site by the western coast, in fact an old harbour sitting in isolated splendour. Remains found in the site include a Temple dedicated to *Dictynnea Artemis*, walls of houses, reservoirs, tombs etc, mainly of the Hellenistic and Roman periods.

Some of the finds are on display at Hania Museum and include vases, terracottas and black-figured pottery of the 6th century BC.

POLYRRINIA — An inland town, south of Kissamos *(Kastelli)* which served as its port. There is not much to be seen, although excavated places include a Temple and the Akropolis with Archaic and Classical remains. Most of the ancient buildings were destroyed for the erection of Venetian and Turkish houses. It had its own mint and worshipped the *Dictynnean Artemis*.

MONASTERIES

MONI GOUVERNETO — Situated within an isolated landscape, to the north of Ayia Triada and takes about an hour to reach on foot. A fortified monastery dating back to 1548 and believed to have been established by a local hermit **St. John of Gouverneto** and the Saint's day is celebrated on October 7th with a fair. It was twice burnt down by the Turks. However the elegant Venetian church survived.

In a short distance to the north, hidden in a wild gorge is the original and oldest monastery in Crete believed to be founded by early Christian hermits and was called *"KATHOLIKO MONASTIRI"*. It was attacked and destroyed by African pirates in the 16th century and the monks moved it to a safer place, now the Gouverneto Monastery.

AYIA TRIADA MONI - *17km from Hania.* One of the most important in Crete, the monastery was founded in 1612 by Venetian Orthodox brothers and monks **Tzagarola** and it is situated in picturesque scenery, a sheltered position at the foot of limestone hills.

The architecture has a strong Venetian influence. The entrance is of classical style dated to 1632 and the belltower to 1650.

It was used by the Venetians as a cultural centre and it is now a training school for Orthodox priests. There is an excellent library containing some 700 volumes and a collection of rich religious relics and objects; however, the monastery is in decline.

The Monastery of Ayia Triada.

25

MONI GHONIA — *24kms to the west of Hania* - A beautifully located monastery overlooking the bay, it is also known as *MONI ODYGISTRIAS* and was founded around 1618, built in a fort-like style for protection. Venetian influence can be seen in most buildings and at one time it was the richest monastery in Crete. It houses an important collection including post Byzantine icons of the 16-17th centuries, in particular, those painted by Paleokapas.

In the years of occupation it played a prominent role as a centre of revolution and was burnt down by the Turks several times.

An International Orthodox Academy has been added recently and organises international theological conferences. A large fair takes place on 15 August.

MONI KHRYSOSKALITISSA - *72km from Hania, along the western coast* - this Nunnery is located on a rocky coastal promontory of a very mountainous landscape, called by the locals as the *"Switzerland of Crete"*. It has however, an almost tropical appearance and it is also noted for the chestnut trees.

The Nunnery is not easily accessible; the trip is long and tortuous, however, those wishing to explore the area will be rewarded. It is dedicated to the Assumption of the Virgin Mary and celebrations take place on 15 August.

The name derives from a tradition and legend that one of the ninety steps to the top of the rock is made of Gold. However, only those who have committed no sins can actually see it. Unfortunately, the number of nuns has dramatically declined

KHRYSOPYGI MONI — This monastery was established around 1400 by a rich Cretan family called *Chartofylaka* and it proceeded to flourish. It was restored in 1608 by another member of the family but it was again destroyed by the Turks in 1821.

It was rebuilt as a fortified castle for protection. The church of the *"Source of Life"* is situated in the middle. There is a library with some 300 volumes, some important documents and a collection of religious objects.

Khrysoskalitissa Monastery in beautiful surroundings.

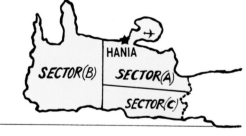

HANIA DISTRICT— COUNTRYSIDE
(NOMOS HANIA)
We divided this into 3 sectors:

SECTOR (A) — Covers the area around Hania, to the south, east and west and Akrotiri Peninsula.

SECTOR (B) — Covers the western side of the district and the coastline.

SECTOR (C) — Covers Lefka Ori mountains and the southern coast.

SECTOR (A) — NORTH & NORTH EAST

KOURNAS - **Lake Kournas** is to the north of the village of Kournas, a rich agricultural area. This is the only lake in Crete with fresh water and was known in ancient times as Korion or Korishia. It comes from a legend of the ghost of a young girl *(Kori)* who was raped by her father along the lake. Locals believe that the lake is bottomless but is still a mystery how such a lake was created.

SOUDHA BAY — A well protected natural harbour, one of the best in the Mediterranean. Here, Greek, American and Nato naval forces are stationed and photography is strictly forbidden in most places.

In the entrance to the bay is the tiny island of SOUDA, a fortified post. Here the Venetians held out longer against the Turkish invasion than any other place in Crete but it was finally taken in 1715.

ALIKAMBOS — The interesting church of PANAYIA has superb frescoes dating to 1315-16 and they are the work of Ioannis Pagomenos, a famous artist of western Crete.

GEORGIOUPOLIS — It was named after Prince George who served as the first High Commissioner in Crete. It has a fine beach and hotel accommodation. Close to the north is the ancient Hellenistic site of AMFIMALLA. Tel. Centre (0825) 22363.

KALAMION — A small fishing village by the southern entrance to Souda Bay and north of the ancient site of APTERA. The Turkish fortress **IZEDIN** was originally Venetian and was taken by the Turks in 1715. It was strengthened and used by them to guard the entrance to Souda Bay. Now it is a prison but is still called Izedin.

SOUDA this is the commercial harbour of Hania and has grown since the end of the 2nd World War. Regular boat and ferry services connect Souda (Hania) with Piraeus and other places. Nearby are the Naval administration and residential buildings and a Greek Naval Hospital.

Nearby is the British and Commonwealth cemetary commemmorating those who lost their lives during the Battle of Crete.

South of Hania

THERISO — This is the village of Venizelo's mother. Here he established his party in 1901 to seek Union with Greece and in 1905 he formed an assembly which resulted in a rebellion. Outside the village is **SARAKINA CAVE** where finds were discovered dating from Neolithic, Minoan and Geometric periods. Tel. Police (0821) 93275.

Above: General view of Soudha Bay — old engraving.
Below: Venizelos Tombstone. From here one gets a panoramic view of the town of Hania below.

27

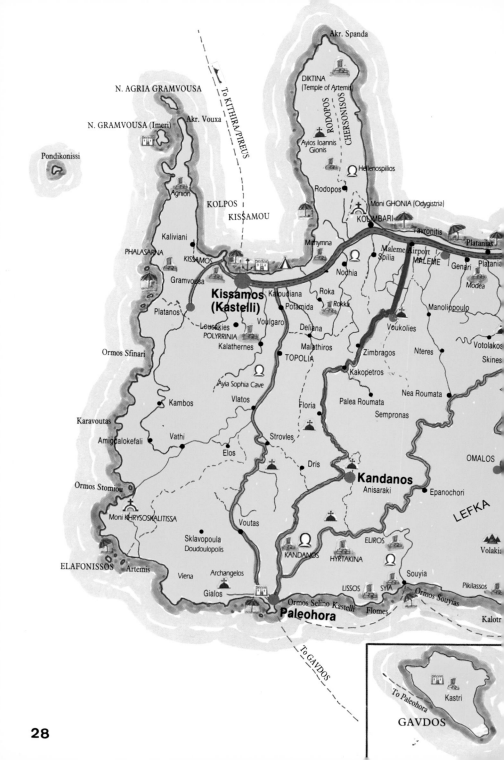

N. AGRIA GRAMVOUSA

N. GRAMVOUSA (Imeri)

Akr. Vouxa

Pondikonissi

To KITHIRA/PIREUS

Akr. Spanda

DIKTINA
(Temple of Artemis)

RODOPOS
CHERSONISOS

Ayios Ioannis
Gionis

Hellenospilios

Rodopos

Moni GHONIA (Odygistria)

Agnion

KOLPOS
KISSAMOU

KOLMBARI

Tavronitis

Kaliviani

Mirhymna

Platanias

PHALASARNA

KISSAMOS

Maleme Airport
Spilia

MALEME

Genari

Platania

Gramvousa

Noghia

Modea

Kissamos
(Kastelli)

Kaloudiana

Roka

Manoliopoulo

Platanos

Potamida

Rokka

Voukolies

Votolakos

Lousakies
POLYRRINIA

Voulgaro

Deliana

Zimbragos

Nteres

Skines

Kalathernes

Malathiros

Ormos Sfinari

TOPOLIA

Kakopetros

Ayia Sophia Cave

Nea Roumata

Kambos

Vlatos

Floria

Palea Roumata

Sempronas

Karavoutas

Vathi

Strovles

OMALOS

Amigdalokefali

Elos

Dris

Kandanos

Ormos Stomiou

Anisaraki

Epanochori

Moni KHRYSOSKALITISSA

LEFKA

Voutas

ELIROS

Volakia

Sklavopoula
Doudoulopolis

KANDANOS

HYRTAKINA

ELAFONISSOS

Artemis

Viena

Archangelos

Souyia

Pikilassos

Gialos

LISSOS

SYIA

Ormos Souyias

Kalotr

Ormos Selino Kastelli

Flomes

Paleohora

To GAVDOS

To Paleohora

Kastri

GAVDOS

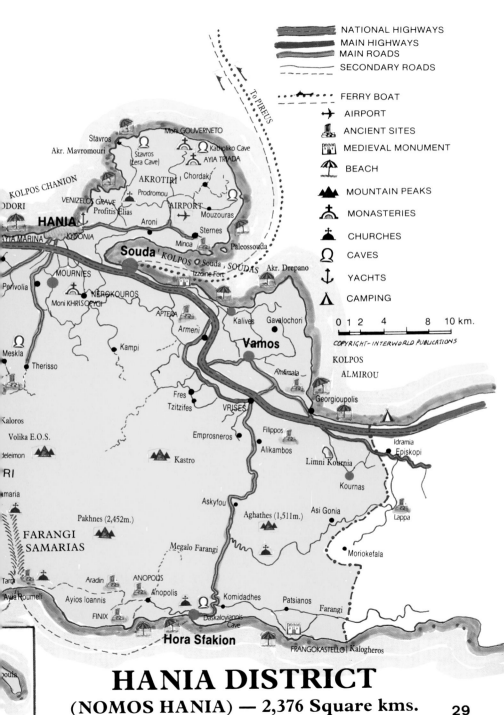

Legend:

- NATIONAL HIGHWAYS
- MAIN HIGHWAYS
- MAIN ROADS
- SECONDARY ROADS
- FERRY BOAT
- ✈ AIRPORT
- 🏛 ANCIENT SITES
- MEDIEVAL MONUMENT
- 🏖 BEACH
- ⛰ MOUNTAIN PEAKS
- ⛪ MONASTERIES
- ✝ CHURCHES
- Ω CAVES
- ⚓ YACHTS
- Λ CAMPING

0 1 2   4   8   10 km.

COPYRIGHT-INTERWORLD PUBLICATIONS

To PIREUS

Stavros
Akr. Mavromouri
Moni GOUVERNETO
Stavros (Zera Cave)
Katholiko Cave
AYIA TRIADA
Chordaki
KOLPOS CHANION
AKROTIRI
Prodromou
ODORI
VENIZELOS GRAVE
Profitis Elias
AIRPORT
Mouzouras
HANIA
Aroni
Sternes
AYIA MARINA
KYDONIA
Minoa
Paleossouda
Souda
KOLPOS Souda
SOUDAS
Akr. Drepano
Izzdine Fort
MOURNIES
Perivolia
NEROKOUROS
Moni KHRISOKYGI
APTERA
Kalives
Gavalochori
Armeni
Vamos
Meskla
Kampi
KOLPOS
Therisso
Amfimala
ALMIROU
Fres
Tzitzifes
VRISES
Georgioupolis
Kaloros
Emprosneros
Filippos
Volika E.O.S.
Alikambos
Idramia
deleimon
Episkopi
Kastro
Limni Kournia
RI
Kournas
amaria
Askyfou
Asi Gonia
Pakhnes (2,452m.)
Aghathes (1,511m.)
Lappa
FARANGI
SAMARIAS
Megalo Farangi
Moriokefala
Tara
Aradin
ANOPOLIS
Ayia Roumeli
Ayios Ioannis
Anopolis
Komidadhes
Patsianos
FINIX
Daskaloyiannis Cave
Farangi
Hora Sfakion
FRANGOKASTELLO
Kalogheros
oula

HANIA DISTRICT
(NOMOS HANIA) — 2,376 Square kms.   29

MOURNIES– A pleasant picturesque village, where the famous Cretan statesman VENIZELOS was born. A garden paradise with large trees, fruit trees and spring waters.

MESKLA — The real "GARDEN OF GREEN", is west of Theriso. A prosperous area with orange groves and vegetable gardens. There are springs and fountains and the river runs with water even during summer. During the Venetian period it was a main agricultural and administrative centre, but also the centre of a revolution against them, headed by a native leader Kantanoleon. The church of the Transfiguration has 14th century frescoes. A chapel outside the village is built over a Temple of Venus *"Temple of Pandimos Aphroditi"*. The ancient site nearby is called **RIZENIA** but very little has come to light apart from Cyclopean Walls and rock cut tombs and chambers.

AKROTIRI — a peninsula rich in history.

THE HILL OF PROFITIS ELIAS provides a superb view of the city of Hania and the surrounding coastline. The **VENIZELOS TOMB** is here and it has become a place of pilgrimage to most Greeks.

The Hill is symbolic of Cretan struggles. In 1897, Cretan insurgents raised the Greek flag expressing their desire to Unite with Greece. This was against the wishes of the European powers and, when a shot fired from the fleet destroyed the flagpole, a Cretan stood on the spot holding the flag. Because of this the sailors refused to fire.

AYIA TRIADA — Moni Gouverneto (Katholiki) are described under Monasteries.

KATHOLIKO CAVE — It is close to the abandoned Katholiko monastery. A formidable cave with a large chamber some 150 metres long and 20 metres in height with many stalactites.

STAVROS — It is situated at the north-western point of Akrotiri. Above the isolated beach is the cave of **LERA,** an ancient sanctuary dedicated to Acacalli, mother of Kydon. It was the setting for part of the filming of ZORBA THE GREEK — the scene when a cable was used to transport wood down the sea.

STERNES — A village to the southern part of Akrotiri near the international AIRPORT, has a fine church of *Ayii Pantes*. Next to the other church of the Annunciation are the remains of a late Minoan house and structures and catacombs from the early Christian era.

PORTRAIT OF VENIZELOS

ELEFTHERIOS VENIZELOS (1864-1936. Born in Mournies (Crete) on 23 August 1864) he gained public notice by his part in Crete's Uprising against Ottoman rule in 1897. In October 1910 he became P.M. of Greece. The most prominent Greek politician and statesman of the early 20th century; through his diplomacy he considerably expanded Greece's territory.

The *"Maker of Modern Greece"*, as Venizelos was rightly called, died in Paris on 18 March 1936.

West of Hania

AYII THEODORI ISLAND — Just of the coast, west of Hania, this small island wa the site of ancient **AKYTOS**. Both Venetian and Turks used the island for militar purposes and a garrison was stationed ther at times. The only inhabitants are now th wild goats *(AGRINI)*, however, only a few c these now remain.

The coast along the western side of Hani provides excellent beaches and has numerou hotels and tavernas.

SECTOR (B) WESTERN SIDE

Most of the area, mainly to the north and western regions is very mountainous and isolated, with rough terrain, primitive landscapes and unexplored ruins. This is in contrast to the rich agricultural land which is situated to the eastern side, south of Kastelli. It is an extremely interesting region for those wishing to explore unspoiled places.

MALEME — Best known for being the centre of the "Battle of Crete" in May 1941. Fierce fighting took place in and around the aerodrome — the first airborne invasion in history. However, the Germans managed to secure a foothold which became the main base for the occupation of the remainder of Crete.

RHODOPOU PENINSULA — A very mountainous peninsula without any proper roads. The central ridges rise to 750 metres and the widest part is 8km across. In ancient times it was known as **CAPE TITYROS** and by the locals it is called *"AKRODIRI SPATHA"* *(Sword Cape)*.

ELLINOSPILLIOS CAVE — On the eastern side of Rhodopou peninsula. It is a long cave with corridors, stalactites and stalagmites and pools. Finds in the cave indicate that it was used by people as far back as the Neolithic Age.

DIKTINA — An ancient site at the top of the peninsula, named after the *Goddess Diktina.* The legend tells us that Nymph Dikina (Britomartis or Artemis) threw herself into the sea to escape from the lustful Minos and was saved by the nets of fisherman.

A Hellenistic Temple was built here to honour her, which was replaced by a Roman Temple in the 2nd century AD. The best way to reach the spot is by boat.

ST. JOHN GIONIS — On the eastern side of the peninsula. The church, which is reached with a truck road, is the centre of a large religious festival which takes place every August 28-29. It is the most important in the region.

SPILIA — A village south of the peninsula, known for the church of *OUR LADY* with its fine 14th century frescoes of the Cretan school. Near the village there is a cave with a natural interior. A feast on October 7th observes the death of St. John the hermit.

Platanias Beach, one of many along the coast, west of Hania.

31

KASTELLI (KISSAMOU)

KASTELLI is the new name of the old city of KISSAMOS, by which name it is still known (by some). It was an autonomous Post-Minoan settlement and was still an important city under the Romans. In the early Christian period it was an Episcopical seat. Under the Venetians it was the see of a Catholic Bishop and became a thriving port. It was fortified in the 16th century.

However, not much remains from the past. Most of the ancient city was covered by later developments. Some excavations revealed various structured baths and aqueducts but none of any significance. All the finds, including a fine mosaic, are housed in the small museum which is situated by the main square, but you may not always find it open.

KASTELLI is a small town with a harbour, mainly for fishermen but also with a weekly boat connection to Southern Peloponese and Piraeus. It can be used as a centre to explore the surrounding countryside. There is a beach and a number of hotels. It is also connected with Hania by a good highway.

Tel. Code: 0822

Tel: Police	22115	Town Hall	22068
Customs	22024	Health Service	22008

POLLYRRINIA

POLLYRRINIA — An ancient settlement (see under Archaeological sites), commanding an excellent view of the Bay of Kissamos and the surrounding areas. It can be reached after a 20 minute climb from the village. The church of the 99 FATHERS was built on materials from the ancient site.

CAPE VOUXA

CAPE VOUXA — This ancient mountainous, narrow peninsula of Korykia is virtually deserted and can be reached only on foot or by boat. At the top western side are two islets: AGRIA (Wild), GRAMVOUSA and IMERI (Tame) GRAMVOUSA. They are inaccessible and were one of the oldest lair of the Mediterranean Pirates. The Venetians established a garisson and a fort which was one of the last three to hold out against the Turks, capitulating only in 1692.

The fort which is on Imeri Gramvousa is in fair condition and can be reached by hiring a boat; if you do so, enjoy also the fascinating coastline. Stop at AGNION to explore the Doric site with a shrine to Apollo and to the north west, near Imeri Gramvousa, there is the fine Coral-red beach of TIGANI BALOS.

A beautiful landscape at Sunset in Western Crete

A view of Paleohora harbour.

TOPOLIA — South of Kastelli, this is a beautiful village. The cave of **Ayia Sophia** nearby has fine stalactites. Around Topolia there are remains of the Neolithic, Minoan, Classical, Hellenistic and Roman periods but very little is to be seen.

KOUNENI — The church of **Ayios Yeoryios** outside the village has early frescoes dating to 1284 with some later restorations. Another church **Michael Archangelos** has early 14th century frescoes.

SELINOS PROVINCE — The south-western corner and one of the most isolated parts of the island it is the centre for the production of fine olives and good olive oil. The area is scattered with many ancient sites and historical monuments from the post-Minoan period, Roman, Byzantine and Medieval although none are very spectacular.

ELAPHONISSOS ISLAND (*Deer Island*), narrow and flat it is south of the Monastery of Khryssoskalitissa (*see monasteries*). Juniper grows by the sandy shores.

PALEOHORA — This is the centre of the southwestern coast and is connected with Hania via Kandanos by a regular bus service. Once it was known as '*the pride of the Libyan sea*'; It was also known as "**KASTELL SELINOU**" where there was a Venetian Fort. The fort was built on the promontory in 1279 and to enter it you go through the church.

The climate here is excellent and the mild winter is ideal for swimming. The beach is outstanding.

It is an ideal centre to explore the mountainous but beautiful countryside and coastline. There are beaches to the western side of the bay and also some hotel accommodation.

Telephone Code: (08231)

Community:	41236
Health:	41211
Customs:	41214
Police:	41207

THE AREA AROUND PALEO-HORA provides many ancient sites: **HYRTAKINA** to the North east. **ELIROS** further to the east is the most important ancient city of the region and it flourished under the Romans and Byzantines. It was the seat of a Bishop but was destroyed by the Saracens in the 9th century AD. **SOUYIA** is a coastal fishing village to the south of Eliros. It is popular with adventurous holidaymakers and the site of ancient SYIA with remains of baths, an aqueduct and some mosaics. **LISSOS** is west of Souyia, by the FLOMES peninsula. There are remains such as the Asklepeion, a Temple containing mosaic floors and a theatre which came to light in recent years.

The route along the main road Paleohora-Maleme-Hania is scenic.

33

General view of Ayia Roumeli Beach.

KANDANOS — A prosperous centre with lots of olive groves. It was a centre of resistance against the Germans who destroyed most of the village. It was restored after the war. In and around the village there are numerous churches including **Ayia Anna, Ayia Paraskevi and Ayios Yeoryios** some containing fine frescoes.

FLORIA — The church of **Ayii Pateres** and **Ayios Yeoryios** is a 15th century fine church and contains good frescoes.

VOUKOLIES — A prosperous agricultural town, the centre of the region with a popular Saturday market. It was also an agricultural centre during the Venetian era. The church of **Ayios Constantinos** is interesting.

SECTOR (C) —
SOUTH & SOUTH EAST

OMALOS PLAIN — It covers 25 sq. kms. and it is about 1000 metres in height. It is one of Crete's most impressive upland plains, looks like an enormous drained lake and after a heavy rainfall, it gets marshy. It is ideal place for the cultivation of cereals and potatoes.

LEFKA ORI *(WHITE MOUNTAINS)* – One of the two highest mountain ranges of Crete. The highest point is **Pachnes** reaching around 2,460 metres (8,080 feet above sea level). An isolated range without roads and the only way to explore it is from the Omalos area to the west, Hora Sfakion to the south and Therisso to the north. Hikers must be experienced and carry a few days supplies. During the winter months parts of the range are covered with snow.

Lefka Ori covered with snow.

GORGE OF SAMARIA   (FARANGI SAMARIAS)

This Gorge, to the west of Lefka Ori, provides the most spectacular adventure for every visitor. During the busy summer months it can get overcrowded if too many coach loads of people arrive at once. However, for those who explore the whole length, it is a magnificent and unforgettable experience. A two day trip is most advisable as it takes a good 5-6 hours to walk through the gorge one way.

Going by bus as an individual, you reach Xyloskalo from Hania through Omalos. Here is a tourist Pavilion which provides some very limited overnight accommodation. Then you start the downhill walk *(see map).* Once you are

through, you reach AYIA ROUMELI by the sea. Here again there is limited accommodation and at peak times it may be full. From Ayia Roumeli there are regular boat connections with Hora Sfakion to the east. These are regular during the summer months but stop by around 6pm. In early spring and late autumn, services are less frequent and very rare during winter. At Hora Sfakion there are numerous flats, and lower grade hotels for overnight accommodation. From there, you go back to Hania by regular bus.

If you arrive at Xyloskalo early in the morning, you may go through the gorge by early

The Gorge of Samaria.

The Gorge of Samaria.

afternoon, reach Hora Stakion by late afternoon and catch the late bus to Hania, all in one day. This is really for the young and fit!

Going by organised tours — This is the most popular way. Excursions can vary from one to three days. The coach will leave you at Xyloskalo; you then go through with a guide and you are later connected with your coach at Hora Sfakion. Details are given in leaflets obtained from your hotel or the tourist information office.

THE GORGE
SAMARIA GORGE is the largest in Greece and one of the longest in Europe, some 18km long and 3-40 metres wide, varing from place to place. The steep rocky walls on the sides have evolved over many millenia. The source of water is from the White Mountains (Lefka Ori) and after a heavy snowfall the thaw brings more water making it inaccessible during some winter months.

You require trainers, leggings shoes or walking boots. There is plenty of drinking water all along the route.

SAMARIA VILLAGE — mainly deserted.
The Venetian church of **OSIA MARIA** (1379 AD) contains some 14th century frescoes. According to mythology, nymph Britomartis (daughter of Zeus) was born here. It is also said that the nereid Acacalis, wife of Apollo was

worshipped and an oracle of Apollo was at an ancient site of Kaino.

After the church of **Afentis Christos** you go through the narrowest section of the gorge called **SIDEROPORTES** *(Iron Gates)* — Further south, **Old Roumeli** is a deserted settlement. The church of **PANAYIA** *(Our Lady of Ayia Roumeli)* is Venetian from the 16th century with some pre-Christian mosaics nearby. It is believed that it was built over the ruins of Apollo's Temple.

NEW AYIA ROUMELI — Inhabited
mainly by *Sfakians* is now mainly a tourist resort. To the east there are the remains of a **Turkish Fort**. The ancient site of **TARRHA** is near the sea. The settlement is a 5th century BC which continued to flourish under the Romans and early Byzantium. It was an important but isolated settlement with its own mint and a glass factory. Very few remains survive, these include the *Temple of Tarrhanean Apollo*.

The beach is very good and tavernas provide meals and refreshments.

CHAPEL OF ST. PAUL — 1½ hours
walk to the east of Ayia Roumeli, this little chapel is within interesting surroundings. Here, St. Paul is believed to have come ashore to christen some natives.

LOUTRO — A small fishing village to the
east of Ayia Roumeli, is situated within a well sheltered cove, still unspoiled and isolated. The first government of Cretan Revolution met there in 1821 in a preserved house called **"Kangelia Kiverniou"** *(The Chancellery)*.

PHINIX — An ancient site, close to Loutro
which was mentioned by Strabo in his travels. Very little remains except some Roman foundations and an early Christian Basilica.

ARADENA — An isolated place. The church
of **Archangel Michael** with some good frescoes. It dates from the Byzantine period and was built of materials from the Phoenician settlement of **ARADIN.** The ruins include man-made caves and a structure depicting *"the dance of the Hellens"*.

AYIOS IOANNIS MONASTERY — It
is situated near the village of Ayios Ioannis and the church of **Panayia** contains well preserved frescoes. The nearby **Dragon caves** *(Drakolakkoi)* are exciting to explore but dangerous.

ANOPOLIS — An ancient town which
flourished under the Romans and used the harbour of Phinix *(see above)*. At its peak, it had several thousand inhabitants and was controlling the surrounding area. It had its own mint. There are only a few remains including some cyclopean walls.

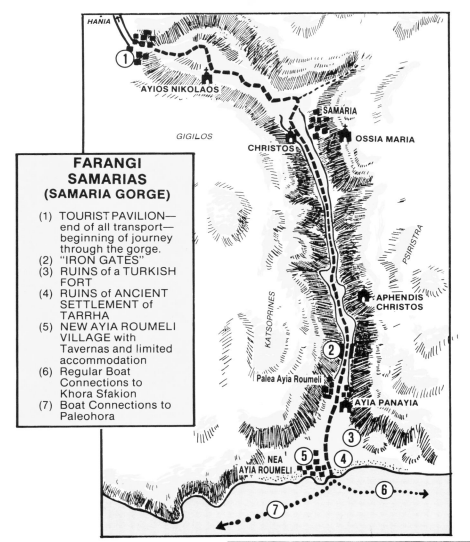

FARANGI SAMARIAS
(SAMARIA GORGE)

(1) TOURIST PAVILION—
end of all transport—
beginning of journey
through the gorge.
(2) "IRON GATES"
(3) RUINS of a TURKISH
FORT
(4) RUINS of ANCIENT
SETTLEMENT of
TARRHA
(5) NEW AYIA ROUMELI
VILLAGE with
Tavernas and limited
accommodation
(6) Regular Boat
Connections to
Khora Sfakion
(7) Boat Connections to
Paleohora

HORA SFAKION — The largest town of the coast. In the 16th century and later was an important commercial port. It was well known for the reputed one hundred churches and chapels scattered all over the area. Over the past few centuries it started a long and painful decline, only to be re-discovered by the tourists, who have given it a new lease of life. Between 28-31 May 1941, over 10,000 British and Commonwealth troops concentrated here and evacuated to Egypt after the fall of Crete but some remained behind and were sheltered by the Cretan resistance fighters.

Hora Sfakion town is the centre of the **SFAKIANS.** Tel. Code: (0825) Police: 91205

Hora Sfakion

37

THE SFAKIAN PEOPLE

A very strong and proud tribe of people, believed to be descendants of the Dorians. They have resisted all forms of domination or influence, Cretan or foreign. Even the presence of the formidable Venetian Castle of Frangokastello did not break their will. The Turks failed too. As an automonous place it was continuously harrassed by the Turks and it was a centre of fierce resistance against the Germans during the Second World War.

At times though, it was a centre of pirates, smugglers and revolutionaries. Vendettas took the lives of many people. The main reasons for the decline however, was immigration during the last century. They lived by resisting everyone; when peace came, there was nothing left for them to fight; so they went to foreign lands, looking for adventure.

THYMNIAN PANAYIA MONI — A

small complex east of Hora Sfakion. Here the self governing Sfakians held their assemblies before 1821.

DASKALOYIANNIS CAVE by the coast.

During the 1770's uprising, **Daskaloyiannis** *(John the Clerk)*, a formidable Sfakian revolutionary used to hide in the cave. He was lured to a meeting with the Turks to discuss a treaty, arrested by trickery, taken to Heraklion and skinned alive.

KOMIDADHES — To the east of Hora

Sfakion. The church of **Ayios Yeoryios** has fine frescoes painted by *Ioannis Pagomenos* who was known to have painted several churches around 1313.

FRANGOKASTELLO — Some 12km

east of Hora Sfakion, it can be reached from Hania by bus. Erected by the Venetians to subdue the Sfakians in the 14th century. Part of the stones were taken from a nearby ancient site which, up to then, was well preserved. It has now disappeared. Many bloody battles were fought around the castle. In 1828 hundreds of Sfakians died defending the fort from a very large Turkish army. The ghost of the defenders, it is claimed, dance at dawn in the middle of May. It is a square castle with a tower of each corner and battlements.

The sandy beach around it is very attractive to many motorists.

View of Frangokastello

CAVDOS ISLAND — It is situated to the south of the district, the south-most territory of Europe, some 50kms offshore and is 37 square kms. It can be reached by boat from PALEOHORA (twice a week — weather permitting). Small boats also run services from Ayia Roumeli, Hora Sfakion and Ayia Gallini during the summer months, taking some tourists.

The island is mainly rocky with steep limestone peaks, but the northern parts provide some isolated but excellent beaches. There are signs of Neolithic and post Minoan habitation around the main settlement of **Kastri**. Some believe that Cavdos was the island described in ODYSSIA as Kalypso's island. It was also mentioned in the ACTS XXVII 16 with the name **CLAUDIA**. In the middle ages it had a much greater number of inhabitants (*several thousand*) and was a see of a bishop. At times, it was also a hideaway for pirates. Now only a few shepherds live here in very primitive conditions without our 20th century amenities.

CAVDHOPOULA (*Chick of Gardens*) 3km long and ½km wide, is a very steep limestone island without any inhabitants to the north of Cavdos island.

HANIA — USEFUL INFORMATION

TRAVELLING AROUND

Communications within the northern part of the Hania district are excellent but nearly non existing on the western coast and non existing at all around Lefka Ori. Southern coastal centres such as Paleohora, Soughia and Hora Sfakion are connected with direct but mountainous roads with the northern centres. Bus communications are excellent in the main centres.

Service Connections with other places:
RETHYMNO-HERAKLION: E. Venizelou St. Bus Station Tel. 23306
KYDONIA REGION (*West & South West of Hania*) Leoforos Kydonias Bus Station Tel. 23257
KISSAMOS & SELINOS REGION (*West & South West*) Leoforos Kydonias Bus Stations Tel. 23052
APOKORONOS REGION (*Eastern District*) E. Venizelos St. Bus Station Tel. 23304
KTEL BUS COMPANY — Leoforos Kidonias Tel. 23052
Sea Connections:
From Kastelli to Peloponese-Pireaes — Tel: (0822) 22024. From Paleohora to Cavdos Island. About 3 trips in the summer — Tel: (0823) 41214. From Hora Sfakion to Cavdos twice weekly in the summer once during winter — Tel: (0825) 91292.

BEACHES OF THE DISTRICT

Some are popular and within easy reach but others are isolated and very difficult to get at. The main popular beaches are west of Hania town including **Kato Stalos, Platanias, Ayii Apostoli, Galatas, Ayia Marina** and **Maleme** where most of the district's top hotels are situated. The whole beach is about 20kms long. To the south, easily accessible are the beaches of **Paleohora, Soughia** and **Sfakia**.

At Akrotiri Peninsula is the beach of **Stavros** and in the east, on the road to Rethymno is **Kalives, Kalami** and **Almyrida**. On the western coast and 59kms from Hania and 17kms from Kastelli is **Falasarna** one of the best

ACCOMMODATION

Hotels and pensions are to be found in all the areas indicated in the map.

A complete list of all hotels and major apartments can be obtained from:

a) The Association of Hotel Owners of the Prefecture of Hania, 25 Daskaloyianni Street — Hania. Tel. (0821) 55395.

b) The National Tourist Organisation of Greece. There is a small number of camping sites and a youth hostel at Hania and further details can be obtained from the National Tourist Organisation or the Tourist Information office of Hania.

CAMPING

AGIA MARINA — (0821) 48555
— Accommodates up to 240 people. By the beach.

DRAPANIAS — (0822) 31444 at Mithimna.
— Accommodates 160 people

KATO DARATSOS — (0821) 51090 West of Hania — Up to 100 people

PALEOHORA at Loubassis
— Accommodates up to 120 people.

FESTIVALS—EVENTS

HANIA VENIZELIA — Annual event with athletic games which take place at Hania Stadium.

HANIA Theatre — Mainly in the Summer with the Cretan Theatre performing at Firga bastion-Hania.

GALATAS — 20-25 May — commemorating the battle of Crete.

KASTELLI — in August; Gramvousa Festival, celebrating a Cretan victory at Gramvousa.

VAMOS — GAVALOHORI-KEFALOS-FRES — July — August — Folklore celebrations, folkmusic, art, dance etc.

SKINES — **Orange Festival** in Spring to the Summer. Folk events.

ELOS — **Chestnut Festival** in October.

KANDANOS — **"Kantania Festival"** of Folklore in the summer.

ARADENA — **Hora Sfakion** — Local Festivities on November 8.

HORA SFAKION — May 20-27 Battle of Crete celebrations.

Above and below: Cretans dancing during their colourful festivals and other events.

RETHYMNON TOWN & DISTRICT

General view of Rethymno from the Castle.

RETHYMNON

Rethymnon is a small picturesque old town with a scenic harbour, a dominating castle and a long sandy beach. The inhabitants are proud of being the most cultural and intellectual people of the island. The University of Crete has its Humanity and Philosophy departments here. Many of the old Venetian houses are listed and restored thus making old Rethymno an attractive medieval place to visit.

An old picture showing the area of Rethymno by the beach. *(From H. Panteris Collection)*

HISTORY

Its history dates from the Late Minoan III period. However, apart from some tombs, everything else has been buried under the town.

It was called, during the classical period, **Rithymna** but was of no great importance neither during the Hellenistic, Roman or Byzantine periods.

It was under the Venetians that the town was enlarged and attracted many intellectuals both from Venice and Crete. There were various local revolts against Venetian rule, however, none were successful. Rethymno was burned and destroyed by the Turkish Corsair Uluc-Ali Pasha in 1571. It was afterwards rebuilt by the Venetians and the fortifications strengthened, including the building of the formidable castle. It was captured after the siege by the Turks in 1646. Various uprisings against the Turks ended with the massive slaughters of 1801 and 1821. In 1897 it was seized by Russian forces acting together with the other western powers to expel the Turks. In 1970 a serious fire destroyed part of the town.

A typical view of old Rethymno.

An old engraving showing the entrance to the Venetian harbour. *(Nicholas collection)*

RETIMO IN CANDIA

PLACES OF INTEREST

1) THE VENETIAN FORT (FOR-TEZZA).

A massive and formidable fortification complex commanding a unique position overlooking the town and the harbour. It was built on a hill to the north of the city. Total length of the outer walls is 1,307 metres and includes 7 bastions, 3 of them to the southern side. It was erected between 1573-1580.

The main gate is to the east and is very impressive. Within the walls there are the remains of various buildings including the CATHEDRAL dedicated to St. Nicholas. It was later converted to a mosque; the church of St. Theodoros, the Residence of the Councillors, the Governor's Residence, the Bishop's Palace. These and others were neglected and fell into disuse or were destroyed by the Turks. Further damage occurred following the German bombing during the 2nd World War.

One can walk all around the castle on the fortifications and the views of the city and the surrounding areas are superb.

2) THE VENETIAN HARBOUR —

Venetian Rethymno required a well protected harbour, safe from the north winds and waves. Work was begun around 1582. The long breakwater to the north of the old harbour in a recent addition.

A very picturesque harbour, crowded with fishing boats; it is closed to traffic. The promenade is full of the tables of restaurants, cafes and tavernas; a romantic spot for a night out. Most of the buildings date to the Turkish periods, only a few from Venetian times.

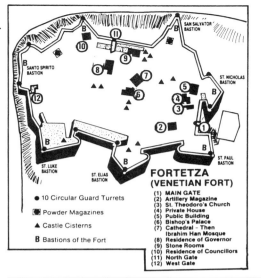

FORTETZA (VENETIAN FORT)

- ● 10 Circular Guard Turrets
- ▢ Powder Magazines
- ▲ Castle Cisterns
- B Bastions of the Fort

(1) MAIN GATE
(2) Artillery Magazine
(3) St. Theodoro's Church
(4) Private House
(5) Public Building
(6) Bishop's Palace
(7) Cathedral - Then Ibrahim Han Mosque
(8) Residence of Governor
(9) Stone Rooms
(10) Residence of Councillors
(11) North Gate
(12) West Gate

Above: Ruins inside the Forteza.
Below: Part of the western side of the walls.

43

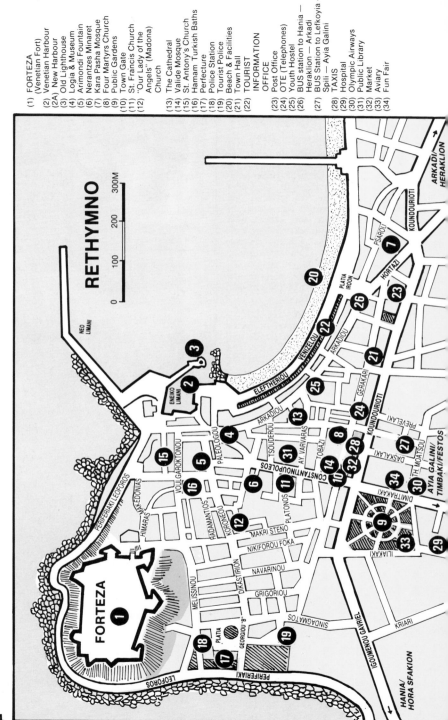

RETHYMNO

(1) FORTEZA
(Venetian Fort)
(2) Venetian Harbour
(2A) New Harbour
(3) Old Lighthouse
(4) Logia & Museum
(5) Arimondi Fountain
(6) Nerantzes Minaret
(7) Kara Pasha Mosque
(8) Four Martyrs Church
(9) Public Gardens
(10) Town Gate
(11) St. Francis Church
(12) "Our Lady of the
Angels" (Madona)
Church
(13) The Cathedral
(14) Valide Mosque
(15) St. Antony's Church
(16) Hamam Turkish Baths
(17) Perfecture
(18) Police Station
(19) Tourist Police
(20) Beach & Facilities
(21) Town Hall
(22) TOURIST
INFORMATION
OFFICE
(23) Post Office
(24) OTE (Telephones)
(25) Youth Hostel
(26) BUS station to Hania —
Heraklion — Arkadi
(27) BUS Station to Lefkoyia -
Spili — Ayia Galini
(28) TAXIS
(29) Hospital
(30) Olympic Airways
(31) Public Library
(32) Market
(33) Aviary
(34) Fun Fair

44

3) THE LIGHTHOUSE to the north east side of the harbour is of the Turkish period and was altered in 1834 and 1844.

4) THE ARCHAEOLOGICAL MUSEUM - *LOGGIA* - It is housed in the elegant Loggia which was built in 1600 and is still the best surviving Venetian building in Crete. It includes a small collection of finds from the district and is expanding slowly as excavations unearth new sites.

Exhibits include Minoan sealstones, ceramics, jewellery, bronze artifacts, vases, idols, sarcophagi, all covering various periods (Minoan, Mycenean, Hellenistic, Classical, Roman).

5) ARIMONDI FOUNTAIN — It has 4 original Corinthian columns and was built by the Venetian Rector Rimondi around 1623-26. It is a very interesting fountain; the best of many surviving ones in the town.

view of the Venetian harbour surrounded with old buildings and scores of restaurants and tavernas.

(6) SANTA MARIA/NERANTZES MOSQUE — A building worth visiting. Originally it was the church of Santa Maria, then became a mosque called "Nerantzes Mosque". The building altered over the years; the impressive minaret was added in 1890. After the departure of the Turks from Crete it became a church, but then housed the music school. Now it is a small Botanical Museum.

(11) ST. FRANCIS CHURCH *(San Francesco)* – One of the most important monuments of the town, the church has now been restored and is used as a civil hall. It houses exhibits from the Venetian period.

(12) CHURCH OF THE MADONA *(Our Lady of the Angels)*. Built during the last years of Venetian rule it was of great importance. Under the Turks, it was allowed to be used by the Christians but was then turned into a mosque. In 1917 it was restored into a church.

(13) THE CATHEDRAL — Dedicated to the Virgin, the Cathedral of Rethymno was built in 1834 on the foundations of an older church. It contains an excellent icon of "Our Lady of the Passion" by an unknown artist. Also there are lovely wood carvings.

The bell tower built in 1889 stands next to the church; an impressive tower, it was built to compete with the minaret of Nerantzes mosque. It was an expensive venture and funds were raised from the inhabitants. The heaviest bell weighs 250 kilos. The building to the south of the church is the Bishop's Palace, a neoclassical building renovated in 1900.

(14) THE GRANDE MOSQUE *(Valide Sultan)* – An early mosque dating to around 1670 dedicated to Sultan Ibrahim Han's mother Valide Sultana. Consists of two large domes and a minaret; a fine monument which may open to the public in the very near future.

(20) THE BEACH – To the east of the harbour, this long sandy beach is ideal for swimming. There are changing facilities and the sea is very good. The beach is several kms long and here one finds most of the hotels, apartments, tavernas and discos.

Walking through the narrow streets, full of bustling commercial life, you will enjoy a flavour of the past with the old Venetian houses, mainly facades and doorways and wooden balconies of the Turkish period.

An old building by the harbour

A view of the Beach from the Castle

ENTERTAINMENT

In Rethymnon town, there are the colourful annual events of The Carnival and the Wine Festival with the numerous evening entertainments. There are numerous cinemas, cafeterias, bars, discotheques and some tavernas with Greek music, but the simplest enjoyment is a stroll along the seafront and a meal by the Venetian harbour during the cool evening.

BUS CONNECTIONS —

Within Rethymnon area:

BUS (1) — Platia Iroon (Heroes Sq.) —
to: Perovolia—Platanes—Camping

BUS (2) — Platia Iroon (Heroes Sq.) —
to: Adele—Loutra

BUS (3) — Platia 4 Martyrs (Sq.) —
to: Armeni

BUS (4) — Corner of Public Gardens —
to: Koube—Atsipopoulo.

KTEL: 22785

Please note: Every effort has been made to supply accurate information but we do not take any responsibility of any differences in addresses, telephone numbers or other information.

USEFUL ADDRESSES (0831)

TOURIST INFORMATION OFFICE (EOT) —
9 Koundouriotou St.   Tel. 29148
TOURIST POLICE — Vasileos Georgiou
  Square...............................28156 .22331
OLYMPIC AIRWAYS — Dimitrakaki St. 22257
ANEK—Steamship Co. 22, 4 Martyron Sq...29846
GENERAL HOSPITAL—Illiakaki Street.... 27491
Ippokration Clinic, 74 P. Koundouriotou St. 29155
Traffic Police 22589
Harbour Police.............................22276
Post Office — 92 Koundouriotou St. 22304
Telephones, Telegrams (OTE)
  15 Koundouriotou Street 134
Archaeological Museum—4 Paleologou St....29975
EMERGENCIES 100
Munincipality 22245
Banks: Bank of Crete 27637
          Bank of Greece.....................23366
          National Bank.......................29271
          Commercial Bank 22288
          Ionian & Popular....................28776

The Rethymno Lighthouse.

47

ARCHAEOLOGICAL SITES

The district has no archaeological sites of great interest to most visitors as the settlements are of lesser importance and there are no impressive remains for the casual visitor. However, they can be very pleasurable to lovers of archaeology.

ELEFTHERNA in the centre of the district 10 minutes walk from the village of Prines. A post Minoan town, it was more prominent in the 8th century BC. One of the most interesting finds, an Archaic torso, now exhibited at Heraklion Museum, room XIX.

The Akropolis stands on a high spot at the end of a sharp ridge and was the main fortification. It was taken over by the Romans who reconstructed it. Towers were added in the Byzantine era.

ARMENI — To the south of Rethymno. A late Minoan Nekropolis. Tombs were cut into natural rock. Some of the tombs are open to visitors. A number of fine painted sarcophagi were found and are on display at the Hania Archaeological Museum.

AXOS – To the north west of Anoyia, a well established centre of the 8th century BC although signs of Minoan III period were found. The ancient Akropolis stands in a commanding position above the village. Finds include relics, bronzes and coins that were minted here in the 8th cent. BC. Some walls and foundations survive.

MONASTERIES

MONI PREVELIS — Situated along the south coast the road goes through the interesting gorge of **Kourtaliotiko.** There is the old Preveli and the new one (Kato Preveli). It was founded by a family from Rethymno in the 17th century and dedicated to *St. John the Theologian.* There is a small library and a museum with religious articles and a fragment of the "True Cross".

It is of some interest to the British tourists for there are several articles including a pair of silver candlesticks given by British officers to thank the local people for their assistance during he Battle of Crete and their evacuation. The monastery was used as a centre for hiding British and Commonwealth officers before their transfer to Egypt but eventually it was discovered by the Germans.

There is a religious feast that takes place on 8 May. The coast nearby is very good for swimming.

MONI ASOMATOS — Situated about 35 kms south east of Rethymno. It was founded in the 10th-11th century. The present structure is of the Venetian period. It was a centre of resistance to the Turkish occupation and thus was destroyed several times. In 1833-60 **Abbot Joseph** established a school and an intellectual centre in the nearby village of **Monastiraki** and Greek culture was taught to the children. It was a very hazardous task. However the school remained in operation until 1913 and was then donated for and used as an agricultural school.

It is set in a picturesque valley of olive groves, vineyards and many trees including planes and dryads.

Close to the monastery is the church of **Ayia Paraskevi** containing some fine wall paintings.

ARKADI

The most famous monastery, symbol of **FREEDOM OR DEATH** to every Cretan. Due to its isolated position it was the centre of resistance against foreign oppressors. In the 1866 revolution, about 1000 Cretan fighters lead by Panos Koroneos together with their families took refuge in the monastery. They were surrounded by a strong Turkish force headed by Mustafa Kyrti Pasha. Faced with humiliation in the hands of the Turks, they decided not to surrender and in a heroic act they blew up the monastery's powder magazine which resulted in

Moni Prevelis.

many deaths. It is estimated that around 500 Turkish troops also died. The event took place on 10 November 1866.

Shock waves of the horrific event spread to all Europe and resulted in the eventual departure of the Turks from Crete, forced to go by the Great Powers.

The monastery, which has been greatly restored is worth a visit. It was originally founded in the 11th century. The facade luckily, remained in its original state and was part of the church of Saints Constantine and Helen. It dates from c1587 when renaissance architecture prevailed in the island with a blend of Gothic and Roman styles. The facade contains a mixture of various styles, including Corinthian columns, classical arches, baroque scrolls and renaissance garlands.

The monastery houses a small museum exhibiting momentoes of the various struggles for freedom.

In the mist of the grove of cypresses stand the sanctuary of the Heroes, where rest the remains of those who sacrificed themselves in 1866.

There is a regular bus connection with Rethymnon. Tel: (0831) Centre 71216.

Arkadi Monastery

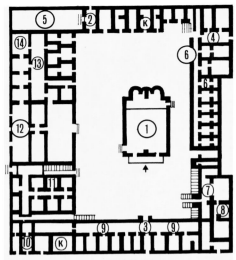

MONI ARKADI

(1) THE CHURCH	(9) CLAOUSTRA
(2) EASTERN GATE	(10) MON GABRIEL'S CELL
(3) WESTERN GATE	(11) GUESTS ROOMS
(4) SOUTHERN GATE	(12) DINING ROOM
(5) POWDER MAGAZINE	(13) CELLARIKA
(6) MUSEUM	(14) OVEN
(7) MESSOKOUMIA	(K) = CELLS
(8) STOA HOUSE	

CRETE
LAND OF THE MINOANS
SECTOR (A)
SECTOR (B)

Written by
RENOS G. LAVITHIS

Edited by
Anna Lavithis and Dr. S. Panteli

First Published in 1988
by Interworld Publications

12, The Fairway
New Barnet
Hertfordshire EN5 1HN

Publisher: Interworld Publications
All rights reserved. No part of this book or any photographs may be reproduced or transmitted in any form in any country, without the permission of the publishers.

ISBN: 0 948853 04 2

Credits to Photographs
The bulk of the pictures are taken by
Mr. Renos Lavithis.
Other contributors are:
Heraklis Panteris, Petros Nikolakis,
Greek Tourist Organisation
Sunvil Travel, S. Papadakis,
Tom Smith, Arthur Gristwood
Howard Lambie and others.
Also Mr. A. Nicholas who provided us with
some excellent maps and engravings from
his medieval collection.

Designed and produced by:
TOPHILL DESIGNS, Barnet, Herts.
Typesetting by:
Sunset Typesetters — London
Colour Planning by:
Cuistance Graphics — London EC1
Printed and bound in Crete by:
G. Detorakis Printing Works,
Industrial Estate, Heraklion.

THE RETHYMNON COUNTRYSIDE

The Rethymnon countryside is both pretty and very contrasting, but mainly mountainous. Being the smallest district of Crete it will be easily explored especially for those staying at Rethymnon.

SECTOR (A) NORTHERN SIDE

The coast of the Rethymno highway which, in most parts, runs close to the sea.

West of Rethymno.

PRINES — A Venetian centre; remains of the past exist.

ARGYROUPOLI — A beautiful village, once a notable Venetian centre. Site of an aqueduct with some remains visible.

ROUSTICA — The church of **Assumption** contains frescoes and remarkable wood carvings.

East of Rethymno.

PERAMA — The village, the agricultural centre of the area. Near it, but 5 km, is the cave of **Melidoni**.

MELIDONI CAVE — A large cave with chambers of stalactites. A place for worship during the Hellenistic period.

TALOS, a mythological giant, protector of Crete, who went striding around the island 3 times a day and hurled large rocks at invaders who had the temerity to approach the island, was said to live in this cave *(it is part of the saga of the Argonauts)*. Dante used it in his version of the inferno. In 1824 some 300 Cretans took refuge in the cave and were smoked to death by the Turkish army.

ANOYIA

One of the best known villages in Crete a) due to the special type of people *(proud, clever and excellent organisers)* and b) their tragedy during the 2nd World War. After the kidnapping of Kreipe, the German Commander and the use of the village as a hiding place, the Germans retaliated by killing the male inhabitants and razing the village to the ground except the church of **John the Baptist**. Anoyia was rebuilt after the war. It suffered another destruction earlier, by the Turks in 1822.

It is a friendly place situated on a commanding position over 2,390 feet high, an excellent centre of handicrafts, wood carving, pottery and weaving.

More easily accessible from Heraklion via Tilissos, the area can be used as a centre to explore the **IDI** mountains.

Tel: (0834)
Town Hall — 31469, Police — 31204.

Part of the village of Anoyia

INTRODUCTION
ACKNOWLEDGEMENTS

After the great success of our Cyprus and Paphos Tourist Guides, producing a similar one for the glorious and ever friendly island of Crete was not only a top priority, but also an enormous challenge. Visited and admired by all Europeans, Crete attracts large numbers of British and other English speaking people who, we hope, will find in our guide most of the information which interests them. With such a treasured island of history, exciting scenery and golden beaches supplemented by its hospitable people and delicious food, we could easily produce many volumes, therefore we have felt some room for more specialist publications.

But putting this Guide together would have been very difficult without the help of the many Cretans we met and Kamarion throughout Athens, but special thanks must be given to the following:

Heraklis Panteris and his family and Stelios Koutsakis and his family, Petros Nikolakakis and Socrates Aghyori, the numerous Metholis's, the directors of the Museums of Heraklion and Athens and the Director of the Greek Tourism Organisation in London and Athens.

Psiloritis, mountain covered with snow during a heavy winter.

PSILORITIS — mountains, some 2,456 metres high. The scenery from the top is fascinating. You can reach and explore the mountain range and the caves of **Antron** and **Kamares** throughout its about... Kamares village in the south (see under *Heraklion*) which is connected by bus to Heraklion.

Only experienced climbers should try to explore the mountains and the truck roads and passages and if possible take a local guide. Proper clothing is required as even during the summer... Also make sure you have your own supplies of water and basic food, medicine and special footwear and a shelter. During the winter it snows heavily.

At the top there is a 14th century chapel of **TIMIOS STAVROS** and some locals make their way here on 14 September.

For IDEON ANTRON Cave please refer to Heraklion Countryside.

AXOS — A nice village amongst orange groves. A tourist centre attracting organised groups for the times when cultural events occur. These include specially staged Cretan dancing. Close by are the ruins of ancient Axos (see archaeological sites).

ARSANI MONI — Now an agricultural centre, once a monastery founded in the last years of Venetian rule and dedicated to **Ayios Yeoryios**. The church was built in 1880. Nearby is the abandoned chapel of **St. Nicholas**. Finds of the post-Minoan period were discovered.

MARGARITES — A village well known for its fine clay vessels. A Venetian centre; the Byzantine church has some frescoes.

VIRANEPISKOPI — The church of the village was built over a Hellenstic site (*perhaps a sanctuary of Artemis*). A Basilica was built during the ... century, destroyed by the Saracens and rebuilt by the Venetians in the 9th century.

PANORMOS — Small coastal town, site of an ancient cel... and Byzantine port. Ruins of a 5th century Basilica can be seen.

SECTOR (B) — SOUTHERN SIDE

MYRIOKEFALO — An old monastery founded in 1665 by St. John the hermit. The church of **Virgin Mary** contains a miraculous icon of excellent Byzantine style. The monks of history... works in the 18th century. Now is used only as a pilgrimage place with a festival taking place on 8...

PLAKIA — An excellent beach by a small but picturesque resort with hotels, apartments and a hostel. Delicious fish is served in the tavernas.

SPILI — Commanding an impressive view of the surrounding area, buried in large trees and famous for its heads of running water. There is an unusual fountain with 19 heads of lions with water pouring from their mouths. It is the seat of the Metropolis of Lambi and Sfakia areas and the three churches of **Ayios Theodoros, Ayios Yeorylos** and the **Transfiguration of Christ Church** contain good frescoes.
Tel; Community: 22046 / Police: 22027.

KOURTALIOTIKO FARANGI — A long narrow gorge with caves running water and in places excellent scenery.

AMARI PROVINCE — between **Kedros** and **Idi** mountains, with beautiful picturesque scenery, dotted with small villages, churches and chapels. The **YERUKAKI** village is known for its excellent cherries. **Asomatos** monastery is described earlier.

APOSTOLI stands at the northern side of the valley and has a 14-15th century church.

AMARI village, the centre of the district has an interesting church of **St. Anne** with frescoes dating to the 13th century, amongst the oldest in Crete.

VIZARI — near **Fourfouras**. Remains of a large Roman town. A mosaic floor dating to 250-300 AD was discovered and an early Christian Basilica with well preserved foundations exist.

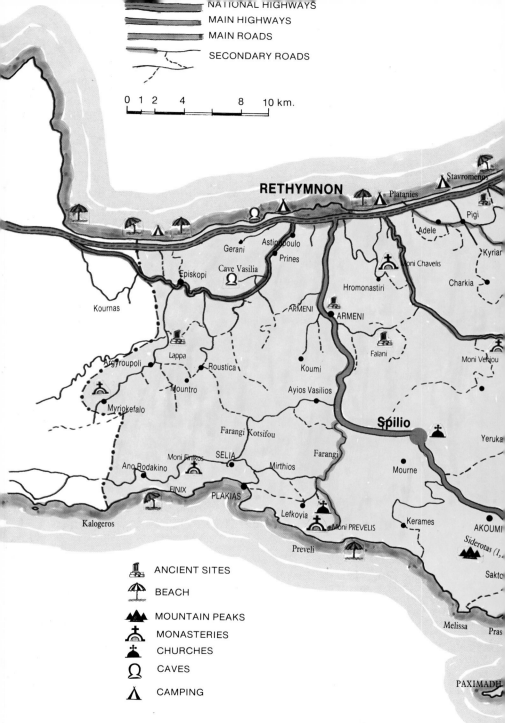

NATIONAL HIGHWAYS
MAIN HIGHWAYS
MAIN ROADS
SECONDARY ROADS

0 1 2   4   8   10 km.

RETHYMNON
Stavromenos
Platanies
Pigi
Adele
Gerani   Astipopoulo
Prines   Kyriar
Cave Vasilia   Moni Chavelis
Episkopi
Hromonastiri   Charkia
Kournas   ARMENI
ARMENI
Lappa   Falani
Argyroupoli   Moni Veniou
Roustica   Koumi
Mountro
Ayios Vasilios
Myriokefalo

Spilio
Farangi Kotsifou   Yeruka
Farangi
SELIA
Moni Finikos   Mirthios   Mourne
Ano Rodakino
FINIX   PLAKIAS
Kalogeros   Lefkoyia   Kerames   AKOUMI
Moni PREVELIS
Siderotas (1,
Preveli   Sakto

ANCIENT SITES
BEACH
MOUNTAIN PEAKS
MONASTERIES
CHURCHES
CAVES
CAMPING

Melissa   Pras

PAXIMADH

RETHYMNON DISTRICT
(NOMOS RETHYMNOU) – 1,496 square kms.

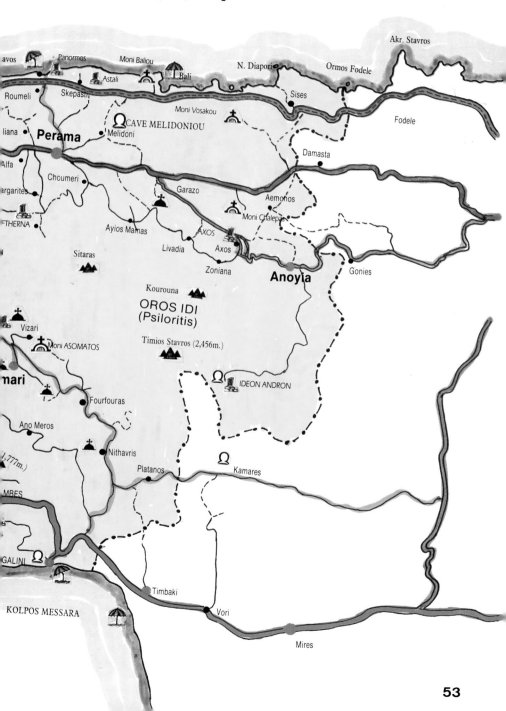

avos
Panormos
Moni Baliou
Astali
Bali
N. Diapori
Ormos Fodele
Akr. Stavros

Roumeli
Skepasti
Sises
Fodele

liana
Perama
CAVE MELIDONIOU
Melidoni
Moni Vosakou

Alfa
Choumeri
Damasta

argarites
Garazo
Aemonos

THERNA
Ayios Mamas
AXOS
Moni Chalepas

Sitaras
Livadia
Axos
Gonies

Kourouna
Zoniana
Anoyia

OROS IDI
(Psiloritis)

Vizari
Timios Stavros (2,456m.)

Moni ASOMATOS
IDEON ANDRON

mari
Fourfouras

Ano Meros

,777m.)
Nithavris

Platanos
Kamares

MBES

GALINI

Timbaki

KOLPOS MESSARA
Vori

Mires

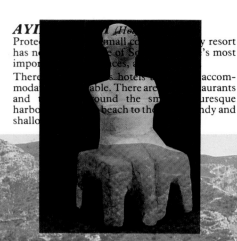

AYI... *(He...)*

Prote... small co... y resort
has ne... e of So... 's most
impor... ces, a...

Ayia Galini is an ideal centre from which to
explore both the coast... ...nd the rocky

There... s hotels ... accom-
moda... able. There are ... aurants 91210
and ... ...ound the sm... uresque
harbo... beach to th... ...ndy and
shallo...

Left: Marble figurine. *Right:* Gold Necklace *(Both courtesy Heraklion Museum)*

The Minoan Civilization

Around the year 3000BC copperworking was introduced; this produced a **Bronze Age** culture which is called the **MINOAN CIVILIZATION**, after the island's legendary ruler **MINOS**. Following the work at Knossos of great archaeologist Sir ARTHUR EVANS, it is now widely accepted that the Minoan Age can be divided into 3 periods, which is called **Early, Middle and Late Minoan** with each having three sub-periods. The whole period in question spuns from around 2600BC to 1050BC with the *Subminoan Age* stretching to 950BC.

During the three phases of the **EARLY MINOAN** (c2600-2300BC) some clearly marked social changes were taking place. The island's

Above: The long beach of Ayia Galini

population increased rapidly as immigrants came to **Palaikastro, Mohlos** and **Gournia** from Asia Minor and the Cyclades and in the Messara there is evidence of new arrivals from Libya and Egypt who settled in many places in the plain. For the first time the population began to leave the open country and to concentrate in villages and towns, and the purely pastoral society declined. Instead of each family making what it needed in wood, pottery and metal, the crafts became specialised: men whom Homer called "Demiourgoi" *(Creators)* set up as specialists and professionalism in craft and art was born. Moreover, the architecture of private houses, also advanced greatly.

By about 2000BC "Palaces" began to be built on the sites of **Knossos, Ayia Triada, Festos and Malia**, inaugurating the **MIDDLE MINOAN** (to c1600BC) or *Protopalatial Period*. Economic, political and social organizations began to flourish, with increased trade in the eastern Mediterranean while stone carving, gold work, jewellery and pottery demonstrated aesthetic progress.

Around the year 1700BC one of Crete's periodic earthquakes destroyed parts of the three major palaces but there was no break in the continuity of Minoan culture. The palaces were reconstructed and even enlarged introducing the *Middle Minoan III* or *New Palace* ... ...these ambitious complexes, with a medley of ... frescoes, paintings, pottery and metalwork are still visible today. Meanwhile Crete ... traded with countries as far as Spain ... ...were massive. However by ...2000BC the ... Greeks had assured an influential, perhaps dominant ... Minoan affairs.

RETHYMNON — USEFUL INFORMATION

TRAVELLING AROUND

An excellent road network connects Rethymnon with all the other northern Greek coastal towns. Plakias, Ayia Gallini and the Amari valley to the south are also well connected to the northern coastal areas. Fairly good roads connect most villages.

Bus Stations to other places on the itinerary:

To: HANIA—HERAKLION

To: Southern Coast (Ayios Vasilios)

To: East and South East (Arhanes)

TAXI stands: 4 Martyrs Sq., Titou Sq., Heroes Sq.

From: AGIA GALLINI there is in the summer daily boat connections with Matala (Tel. 91206)

BEACHES OF THE DISTRICT

Along the northern side, the main beaches are concentrated to the eastern part of the town and further east there is a long stretch of up to 10 miles around the **Platanies** and **Stavromenos** areas. Further east are the beaches of **Lavris** and **Bali**. To the western side, long and narrow stretches of beaches are parallel to the main Rethymnon-Hania highway.

To the south coast, the most popular is that of **Ayia Gallini** and further west are the protected bay and beach of **Plakias** and **Preveli** beach close to the monastery.

ACCOMMODATION

Most of the accommodation along the northern coast is to the east of Rethymnon along the sandy beaches. To the south the main centre is Ayia Gallini. For a complete list of all accommodation please contact the Greek National Organisation or ASSOCIATION of CRETAN Hoteliers—Dedalomenos and Malikouti Street, Heraklion Tel. 222967, Telex 262380 or the municipality of Rethymnon.

CAMPING SITES ARE:
Elizabeth — 3km east of Rethymno
Tel. 28694 — Up to 500 people
Arcadia — 4km east of Rethymno
Tel. 28825 — Up to 150 people
Also at Ayia Gallini (0832) 91386 and Plakia.

Geometric, Hellenistic & other Periods

Crete still played a part in the transfer of various cultural forms from the Near East to Greece. Before the Roman conquest of 67BC, Crete went through the so-called **Protogeometric: 950-800BC**, **Geometric: 800-700BC**, **Hellenic 700-550BC** and **Hellenistic 550-67BC** Periods. Though there is no more elaborate palace architecture, building techniques survived, as we know from the evidence of tombs, and there were fresh innovations in pottery. However, in those troubled times of transition, some of the native population took to the mountains and built settlements of refuge for themselves in high places such as **Karphi**, **Kavousi** and **Vrokastro**. Nevertheless, the increasing use of iron by the beginning of the 10th century contributed to the formation of smaller separate city-state communities and the centralised uniformity of Late Minoan times. Similarly, the growth of iron-working led to the closer attachment of domestic industry to agriculture, resulting in an increasing number of village producers independent of markets.

By the beginning of the 8th century BC conditions in Crete had become more settled and a few old Minoan sites like **Ayia Triadha**,

55

HERAKLION TOWN

General view of Heraklion at sunset

It is the 5th largest city of Greece and Crete's most renowned. It is the centre of government administration, the centre of all transport, buses, air and car ferries. Also for commercial activity and artistic events. A town for everybody to enjoy, a mixture of old Venetian, Ottoman and early century influences, combined together with modern architecture.

An old photo of Heraklion Harbour and Castle. *(H. Panteris Collection)*

HISTORY

Not much early history has been recorded. Only a few tombs from the Minoan period have been discovered on the east side of the town. Strabo mentioned Knosso's harbour as **HERAKLE-IUM** (*Hercules Seventh Labour*). Nothing though remains of any Hellenistic or Roman presence. In the early Christian years there was a small settlement with a fort and was called **KASTRO**.

When the Arabs took over the island in 824 they enlarged the town as well as the fort which was called RABDH-AL-KHANDAK and by the locals **KHANDAKI** (*Castle of the Moat*). When the Arabs were driven out, the castle and the town was called **KHANTAX**. When the Venetians took over Crete, Khantax was renamed **CANDIA** (a name which the Venetians gave also to the whole island).

It soon became a centre of Venetian power and an influential sea port. Fortifications were erected, amongst the strongest in the world. It took the Turks nearly 22 years and a long and bloody siege to take over the fort in 1669. Even under the Turks, the Europeans continued to call the city CANDIA and the Cretans as to MEGALO KASTRO (*The Big Fort*). In 1922 it was officially adapted as **HERAKLION**.

Its large port and airport bring in most of the tourists entering Crete and it's also the gateway to **KNOSSOS,** one of the most famous ancient sites of the world.

A General view of Koules the Venetian Castle.

An old Venetian Print showing a naval siege of Heraklion. *(Nicholas collection)*

(1) HERAKLION ARCHAEOLOGICAL MUSEUM

The most popular Museum in Crete and one of the best known in the world. But unfortunately, its popularity attracts so many visitors and for those deeply interested in its vast archaeological wealth and superb board collection, more than one visit is required. It is advisable to be there at opening time or visit it during the off peak season.

The present building was erected in 1937 - 1940 but the exhibits were incompetenly displayed by N. Platon in 1960 and completed by S. Alexiou in March 1964. The whole collection is exhibited in a chronological order and can be easily followed by the visitor. An excellent, official guide, fully illustrated and describing the rooms in detail is available from the museum in most popular languages. Below a very brief description of the museum for basic reference:

Two of the most well known exhibits of Heraklion Museum, to the *left*, the Goddess of the snakes, called 1600 BC — first topless known Lady, and to the right, the head of the 16th cent. BC *(Heraklion Museum)*

Arabic Occupation

The Arabic Occupation lasted from 824-961 AD. For 137 years Heraklion was a stronghold from which Arab pirates from Spain, Africa and Egypt ravaged the coasts and islands of Greece. A slave market was held there which supplied the *Emirs* of the east with the flower of Greek youth and beauty to adorn their courts and fill their harems. The Metropolitan Cyril was martyred when the Roman capital Gortys fell to the Arabs and his cathedral, the church of St. Titus was destroyed. In all nineteen cities are said to have been sacked and only in the mountains (*in places like Sphakia to the furthest of the island*), did a handful of Christians survive.

This period before (*from 824-961 AD*), witnessed a massive depopulation and economic ruin of the island. However, from 825-960 AD, several major expeditionary forces were sent by the Byzantine Emperors to recover Crete from the Saracens. All failed because of the incompetence of the leaders. In 960, however, the island fell to **Nicephorus Phokas**. The Saracen stronghold of Heraklion fell on March 7th.

Second Byzantine Period

The **Second Byzantine Period** (*Eastern Roman Empire*) lasted from **961 to 1204.** The island was ruled by a *Duke of Crete* who was its governor and supreme military commander. The Duke and his staff were in the main chosen from the kin of the Emperor. A form of feudalism seems to have been introduced at this time by the noble families who lived in Crete and by those who settled there. The lands belonging to these families were cultivated by a class of men called 'colony' — who were Christianised Arabs, and by Serfs who were prisoners of war or simply bought slaves.

Heraklion became the civil and religious capital of the island. Furthermore, the Patriarchate of Constantinople restored the church in Crete and retained the names of the bishoprics as they had been before the Arab occupation, although the former metropolitan cities had disappeared. Gortys, Knossos, Arkadia, Ierapetra, Hersonissos, Kydonia, Syvritos, Lappa and Kissamos, were no more, but their bishops lived and worked in other places which often came to be called **"Episkopi"**. The metropolitan of Gortys became Archbishop of Crete and removed to Heraklion where a cathedral was built and dedicated, like that of Gortys to the Apostle Titus, the patron Saint of Crete.

On the whole, the history of Crete from 961 to 1204 was relatively uneventful, except for the seizure of the island by the rebel admiral **Caryses** in 1092. The Cretans took the side of the imperial forces and killed Caryses. It must be noted that the island's population showed a marked upsurge, reaching probably 250,000 in 1204.

By 1200AD the Empire, ruled from Constantinople had so shrunk that there remained only Asia Minor, Thrace, eastern and Central Macedonia, Thessaly, Crete and a few other islands.

Christ's disciples and the Virgin among them observe the Christ Pantocrator blessing them (not in the picture). A wall painting from Panayia Kera *(see page 125)*

NEOLITHIC & PRE-PALATIAL Periods (c6500-2000BC)
The room contains many cases 1–18 in all exhibiting various finds including
Pottery from Knossos, Festos, Lebeb, Messara. Jewellery from Lebeb, Messara,
Arkhanes. Other items include vases, sealstones, tools, terracotta ... with 3 men on the horns.

Venice is contained in the involved politics of the Fourth Crusade, proclaimed by Pope Innocent in 1202. Predominantly a French enterprise, the Fourth ... the Dalmatian coast and then onto Constantinople (*for 900 years this great christian city commanded the trade routes between Asia, Russia and Europe and was the bastion and guardian of christianity*) ostensibly in order to restore to the throne the deposed Angeli rulers,

ROOM II - PROTOPALATIAL Period (c2000-1700BC) - Knossos - Malia Palaces and Peak Sanctuaries

Cases 19-29 ... was Constantinople's ... darker than that Mohammed II ... the Crusaders **Vessels** ... **sealstones** ... (Case 19). was beyond doubt one of the most despicable acts in history.

ROOM III - PROTOPALATIAL Period (c2000-1700BC) - Festos Palace

Cases 30-40 ... "A History of Venice" wrote as ... includes various interesting samples in **pottery, vases, clay idols, altars** and offering tables ... an important ... the period ... are the **pitheres** ... Festos Disc ... all of Europe terracotta disc ... with writing signs on both sides of ough religious significance but it has not been translated yet.

ROOM IV - NEOPALATIAL Period (c1700-1450BC) Knossos - Festos - Malia

This is an excellent collection of Minoan ... 'Those men were transported, under ... the Cross.' ... Dandolo in the name of the Venetian Republic; and ... Venice derived the major advantage from the tragedy, so she and her magnificent old *Cases 44-59* includes **pottery, vases, bronze, swords, domestic tools, sacred relics** etc. Most important is the famed **Snake-Goddess** responsibility for the havoc they wrought upon the world. and a remarkable **bull's head rhyton** (Case 57) from Knossos.

ROOM V - LAST NEO-PALATIAL Period (c1450-1400BC) Knossos

Cases 60-70 – Of all the Levantine possessions acquired by Venice, as a result of the Fourth Crusade, by far the most important was **sealstones**, ... **Egyptian objects**, ... Alexios IV, at the cost of 1,000 marks of silver. Boniface signed the famous document of cession, the *Refutatio Cretae*, and this became the legal root of title by

ROOM VI - NEO-PALATIAL Period (c1700-1450BC)

Cemeteries of Knossos held the island Cases 71-78 – A rich selection of finds from various tombs including **Vases, bronze weapons, a helmet** with boar's tusks (Case 78) the Venetians occupation lasted 204 years ... 86-87) and a **skull and skeleton** of a horse from the Venetians (*were engaged elsewhere*) had time to take possession of the island, their great

ROOM VII - NEO-PALATIAL Period ...

rivals, the **GENOESE**, had established a colony there. Around the From the central ... year 1206, a Count, mainly Meets, ... the Genoese pirate and self-styled Count Khani all ... of Malta, landed an army on the island and occupied Heraklion *Cases 89-102* ... where a Genoese ... column ... **swords** and **double-axes** ... 'honey bees' ... for a Venetian invasion 49 kilos, **gold jewellery** ... of the Museum's masterpieces ... but it wasn't until 1211 ... the Ayia Triada – The **Harvesters Vase** ... **chieftain's cup** ... **Rhyton of the Athletes** (Case 96) ... that the first comprehensive attempt at colonisation was made and the organisation of a Cretan government

ROOM VIII - NEO-PALATIAL Period (c1700-1450BC) N-Kato Zakros

Most spectacular ... society of Crete had a ... military power was in *Cases 103-* ... the hands of the **Duke**, who ... Venetian nobles ... one with ... After the Duke came **ignots** and **councillors** (*Consiliarii*), who were elected in the same manner for two years ...

ROOM IX - NEO-PALATIAL Period (c1700-1450BC) Eastern Crete

Cases 119- The island was ... into six *Sestieri* ... **bronze figures, vases, lamps, idols** ... of Crete from that of the other conquered also **tools and weapons** ... the almost constant insubordination

ROOM X - POST-PALATIAL Period (c1100-1100BC) - Post-Minoan Civilisation

Cases 130- ... of the Cretan population. One insurrection followed another in rapid **goddesses, sacred horns, jewellery, vases, necklaces, bronze weapons,** succession including the **Hagiostephanitais** in 1212 and many from Knossos, Ayia Triada, Festos ... were extremely serious. Other *Case 140* there is an **offering table** ... by Alexios Kallerges in 1283 ... shrines. revolts took place in 1217-19, 1230-36, 1261 and 1364-66.

ROOM XI - SUB-MINOAN, EARLY GEOMETRIC Period (c1100-800BC)

Cases 146-158 - We enter here into a new phase of the history of Crete. Although Minoan influences can be seen, they are not as strong as before.

The exhibits include **vases, votive figures in bronze, clay figures, bronze brooches, gold jewellery, iron weapons, cult objects, statuettes** and a **head of a goddess** *(Case 158)*. Most of the exhibits come from the Prinias and Inatos cave.

ROOM XII - LATE GEOMETRIC & ORIENTALIZING Periods (c800-600BC)

Cases 159-170 - A new area of revival in Crete and this is presented here with the numerous exhibits of unusual **geometric pottery** *(Case 159)*. There are models of **sacred trees with doves from Knossos** *(Case 162)*, **funerary urns** from Knossos, **bronze decorations** from Idea Cave *(Case 169)*, **jewellery, a bronze belt, votives of animals** etc.

ROOM XIII - GALLERY OF MINOAN SARCOPHAGI (c1400-1100BC)

These mainly belong to the post-Palatial period. The collection is interesting and the **sarcophagi** are of different shapes and sizes, found in tomb chambers. Some have interesting reliefs of animals, marine creatures and bull scenes.

ROOM XIV - MINOAN WALL PAINTINGS (c1600-1400BC)

You reach this room from a staircase from ROOM XIII. This is a gallery of the most ancient art (apart from the Egyptian), on show anywhere in the world. These wall paintings *(frescoes)* have been removed from the Palaces of Knossos, Ayia Triada and Amnisos. Some are in their original state and some have been restored. They include masterpieces such as **THE LILY PRINCE, THE BULL'S HEAD, THE DOLPHINS** all from Knossos. **WHITE & RED LILLIES** from Amnisos **WILD CAT & BIRDS, MARINE SUBJECTS, THE CUP BEARER** from Ayia Triada.

In the centre of the room there is *Case 171* exhibiting the most important item of the museum, a **Minoan Sarcophagii** of c1400BC from Ayia Triada showing religious rites for the dead.

ROOM XV-XVI - MINOAN FRESCOES (c1600-1400BC)

Two adjoining small rooms to the north of room XV, exhibiting further Minoan frescoes of smaller sizes including **LA PARISIENNE** and **RITUAL DANCE** —Room XV **DANCING GIRL, BLUE MONKEY, THE LEADER OF THE BLACKS** Room XVI.

ROOM XVII - THE YIAMALAKIS COLLECTION

This collection was aquired in 1962 from Dr. Yiamalakis, a doctor from Heraklion who over the years collected a vast amount of Minoan and post-Minoan art. It is shown in cases 178-191 and includes **bronze statues, jewellery, archaic pithoi**

ROOM XVIII - GREEK & ROMAN MINIATURE ART (including Archaic & Hellenistic Periods

Mainly a collection of **pottery, bronze and clay figurines, coins, jewellery, glass vases, armoury.** From here a staircase leads downstairs to the east wing.

ROOMS XIX and XX - SCULPTURES from the ARCHAIC - CLASSICAL - HELLENISTIC & ROMAN Periods

These two rooms contain, apart from **sculpture; sarcophagii, statuettes, vases,** all beautifully displayed and include items from Presos, Roman Knossos, Paleokastro, Dreros, Gortyna, Prenias, Eleftherna. The collection provides an excellent opportunity for the visitor to observe the development of art during the latest years of ancient Cretan History. Important is the original work of the **Archaic Temple of Prinias.**

Above left: Pithos with double axes from Knossos 15th cent. BC.
Above right: Libation jug found at Katsabas Tombs (1600-1400 BC)
Below: Ayia Triada Sarcofagus showing a bloody sacrifice (c.1400BC) *(Heraklion Museum)*

of 1821 when the men of **Sfakia** rose up in arms to avenge the massacre of 30 Christians at Hania, and the murder of the Metropolitan and five bishops at the Cathedral altar in Heraklion. By the Spring of 1824 the rising was over — partly crushed by the Egyptian troops summoned by the Sultan to help and was incited by the natives of the island of Grabousa, following the defeat of Turkey at the naval battle of Navarino on 27 October 1827 who sent one of their leaders (*the Epirot called Hadji Mihalis*) into Crete to stir up a revolt. He was soon defeated by the Turks at **Frangokastello** in 1828; he was captured and cut into small pieces.

Between 1822, when the Egyptian troops were first summoned to Crete and 1840, the island was governed on behalf of the Sultan by the *Viceroy of Egypt*. In 1830 Egyptian rule received the official sanction of the Great Powers (Britain, France, Italy and Russia) who had taken Crete nominally under their protection. Egyptian rule was opportunistic and oppressive. This rule fell even more heavily upon the Moslems than upon the Christians, the result being that the population of the island which in 1821 numbered 289,000 had shrunk by 1840 to 129,000.

In 1840 Crete once more passed under Turkish control and in 1841 both Christians and Moslems tried to exploit the situation and improve their lot. Whereas the Moslems were content to request reduction in taxation and administrative reforms, many of the Christian leaders demanded union with Greece. Encouraged by the Cretan Committee which had been set up in Athens, the Cretans of the Region of Sfakia (*Sfakiots*) revolted. Yet, although these Sfakiots rose in strength, they were unable to stand up to vastly superior forces. For the next 15 years Crete remained quiet, during which time the Albanian governor ruling on behalf of the Sultan showed more severity towards the Turkish beys than towards the Christians. Faced with heavy exactions, many of the Moslems sold their estates and left the island. As a consequence more and more land passed into Christian hands — a development which had already begun at the time of the Egyptian occupation. What is more, the Christian population of Crete steadily increased. The next major revolt had begun in 1866 and lasted until 1869; this again was only suppressed with the aid of Egyptian troops.

The monastery of ARKADI is long remembered by the Cretans with pride and gratitude and is commemorated by an annual feast on 10 November. After two days intense fighting, the brave defenders, like those of Messolonghi 40 years before, blew up their powder magazines. On this occasion 450 perished along with over 400 Greeks. Arkadi has been, ever since, a symbol of the Island's fight for freedom.

(2) HISTORICAL & ETHNOGRAPHICAL MUSEUM

This interesting museum houses a well displayed collection of all main periods of Cretan History, culture, local art etc. It is housed in the home of **Andreas Kalokerinos**, a student and benefactor of Cretan heritage and culture.

BASEMENT — Here there is a collection of early Christian and Byzantine sculptures and other items, also exhibits from the Venetian and Turkish periods.

MAIN FLOOR — It contains the main collection with early Christian objects from the Basilica of Ayios Titos and Ayii mosaics, frescoes, icons and other religious relics from various monasteries and churches.

AT THE REAR — Along the corridor there are pictorial photographs of the Battle of Crete (Spring 1941). The two rooms are the faithfully reconstructed studies of two famous Cretans, one **NICOS KAZANTZAKIS**, where many of his books and belongings are exhibited. The other is of **EMMANUEL TSOUDEROS**, a great statesman and Prime Minister of Greece from April 1941 to April 1944 in exile.

UPPER FLOORS — These are the rich folk art articles including wood carvings, textiles, embroidery, costumes and a reconstructed Cretan home with its furnishings.

(3) ST. MARKS BASILICA — Built in 1239 and reconstructed ... an impressive Venetian church, it became a mosque under the Turks. It was restored in 1961 and now houses a collection of reproduced frescoes from Byzantine churches all over the island. It is also sponsored by the society of Cretan Historical studies which dates back to the Venetian period, and it is used for exhibitions of arts, crafts, paintings, lectures and concerts.

(4) ST. KATHERINE'S CHURCH – (AYIA EKATERINI) ... the north west corner of the square also of the Ayios MINAS Cathedral ... some years ago and now ... very interesting collection of ... 10th centuries ... including wood carvings, manuscripts ... coes and icons and 6 works of **MICHEL DAMASKINOS**, a well known Cretan contemporary of El Greco. His paintings are of high artistic value ... it is open daily except some afternoons.

Cretan Autonomy and Union with Greece

PLACES TO EXPLORE

(5) THE VENETIAN HARBOUR
The old Venetian Harbour around the Castle is full of colourful fishing and sailing boats.

...

with **Greece.** Today Venizelo's House has become a place of pilgrimage for Cretan patriots.

Eventually, and leaving all details aside, Greece and Turkey signed a treaty on 14 November 1913 in which a common frontier was delineated and Crete definitely assigned to Greece. The island was formally taken over on **14 December 1913** by King Constantine, at whose side were the Crown Prince George *(who never became king)* and Venizelos, the Prime Minister.

British troops stationed in Crete under the Great Powers protection treaty parade at Candia during the Kings Birthday *(H. Panteris Collection)*

(7) VENETIAN HARBOUR BUILD-INGS — These include the **ARSENALI** on the eastern side of the promenade, the great vaulted and arcaded chambers, now restored, were used for the building and servicing of ships. The **WAREHOUSES** to the west, also restored were used to store salt.

(8) VENETIAN WALLS — The Walls dominated the old city of Heraklion. They were erected in the 15th century and strengthened in the 16th century by **Michelle Sammocheli** of Verona in anticipation of a Turkish attack. They were the strongest of any castle in the Mediterranean. Parts of them have survived, have been cleaned and visible in many places. For those enjoying a good walk, they can explore the 4kms long Walls, Bastions and Gates.

There are 7 *(see map)*, in one of which **THE MARINENGO Bastion,** Nicos Kazantzakis was buried *(see below)*.

(9) THE GATES — The original gates were too narrow for modern traffic, so some have been enlarged but are well preserved. They include **PINIGRA GATE** *(PANTOCRA-TOR)* also known as the **HANIA GATE,** dates to 1570 and is the gateway to the south and west of Crete.

GESU GATE *(JESUS)* or *KENOURYIA* = NEW GATE dates to 1587 and is the gateaway to the south and east of the island.

Above: Remains of the old Venetian Arsenali.
Below: General view of Heraklion Harbour with passenger boats in the background.

(10) KAZANTZAKIS TOMB — A very simple tomb on the MARINENGO Bastion from where you can enjoy the magnificent views of the walled city of Heraklion and the surrounding area. Kazantzaki's tomb is very simple but has become a place of pilgrimage for all Greeks.

NICOS KAZANTZAKIS

Known worldwide, as the author of ZORBA THE GREEK. He was a Cretan, one of the best known authors of all Greece and the World. He was born in 1883 and died in 1957. He was the author of many books including Travel Books and some of his novels have been translated into many languages and have been made into films. However, his controversial and somewhat strange philosophy and character contradicted many of the Church's beliefs and ideas; therefore, he was ex-communicated and the church refused to bury him in a cemetery.

So his followers and friends chose the spot overlooking on one side the city of Heraklion and the other side the mountain with the face of sleeping ZEUS *(see picture)*. His grave is a simple cross and tombstone with his own philosophical words,

I HOPE NOTHING
I FEAR NOTHING
I AM FREE

The simple tomb of the world famous N. Kazantzakis.

(11) AYIOS TITOS — The church was named after the Patron Saint of the island. It was an early Greek Byzantine church and was modified by the Venetians in the 16th century, and being converted to a mosque by the Turks. In 1923 it once again became an Orthodox church.

The Church contains a mixture of architectural elements of different periods. In 1966, the holy head (scull) of St. Titos was returned to the church from Venice, where it had been kept for many centuries. The eastern parts of the church contain excellent wall paintings and frescoes, recently restored.

(12) LOGGIA - TOWN HALL — This excellent Venetian Building, now used as the Town Hall, was constructed in the 17th century and was the renowned **LOGGIA**. It is a fine example of Palladian Renaissance style of building.

(13) FOUNTAIN SQUARE — Also known as the **LION'S SQUARE,** is a cosmopolitan square with interesting shops, restaurants and cafeterias all round it. Better known for its fountain which was erected in 1628 and was supervised by governor-general **Francesco Morosini,** the builder of many fountains in Crete. The fountain has 4 lions sculpted, one on each side and at the base there are bas-reliefs of mythical marine animals.

(14) EL GRECO PARK — A small park, but an ideal place to relax. It is popular with local young lovers and tourists. It provides public conveniences and a small playground for children. It is dominated by the bust of El Greco at the entrance.

(15) LIBERTY SQUARE — Part of it is closed to traffic, which makes it an ideal place to sit quietly and enjoy a coffee or a cold drink, after visiting the shops or the nearby Archaeological Museum.

To the west side is **Dikeosinis Avenue** with the Court Houses — Prefecture, which was once the Venetian monastery of **St. Francis.** There are also other government buildings which were used by the Turks as barracks and by the Germans during the war as their Cretan headquarters.

(16) THE MARKET PLACE — One of the most colourful places of Heraklion full of excitement and life with traders using their artistic and selling skills. The market is a long road and mainly in the open air. Here you can buy anything you may wish, souvenirs, clothes, leathergoods, food, wines and spirits, fresh fruit and vegetables. The nearby streets provide some excellent tavernas frequented by locals which guarantees delicious and inexpensive Cretan dishes.

65

HERAKLION

450 M APPROX.

0   150   300

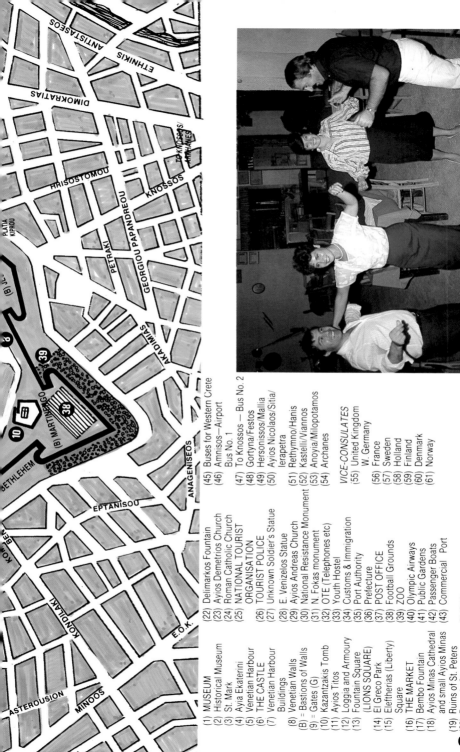

Cretans having a good time in a Heraklion club.

Map street labels: ETHNIKIS ANTISTASEOS, DIMOKRATIAS, HRISOSTOMOU, KNOSSOS, PETRAKI, GEORGIOU PAPANDREOU, IOKNOSSOS/MAHANES, PLATIA KIPROU, AKADIMIAS, (B) JL, ANAGENISEOS, BETHLEHEM, (B) MARTINENGO, EPTANISOU, BENI, KOKKINI, KONDILAKI, E.O.K., MINOOS, ASTEROUSION

(1) MUSEUM
(2) Historical Museum
(3) St. Mark
(4) Ayia Ekaterini
(5) Venetian Harbour
(6) THE CASTLE
(7) Venetian Harbour Buildings
(8) Venetian Walls
(B) = Bastions of Walls
(9) = Gates (G)
(10) Kazantzakis Tomb
(11) Ayios Titos
(12) Loggia and Armoury
(13) Fountain Square (LIONS SQUARE)
(14) El Greco Park
(15) Eleftherias (Liberty) Square
(16) THE MARKET
(17) Bembo Fountain
(18) Ayios Minas Cathedral and small Ayios Minas
(19) Ruins of St. Peters
(20) Panayia Stavrokoros
(21) Ayia Triada Church

(22) Delimarkos Fountain
(23) Ayios Demetrios Church
(24) Roman Catholic Church
(25) NATIONAL TOURIST ORGANISATION
(26) TOURIST POLICE
(27) Unknown Soldier's Statue
(28) E. Venizelos Statue
(29) Ayios Andreas Church
(30) National Resistance Monument
(31) N. Fokas monument
(32) OTE (Telephones etc)
(33) Youth Hostel
(34) Customs & Immigration
(35) Port Authority
(36) Prefecture
(37) POST OFFICE
(38) Football Grounds
(39) ZOO
(40) Olympic Airways
(41) Public Gardens
(42) Passenger Boats
(43) Commercial Port

BUSES
(44) Main Bus Station

(45) Buses for Western Crete
(46) Amnisos—Airport Bus No. 1
(47) To Knossos — Bus No. 2
(48) Gortyna/Festos
(49) Hersonissos/Mallia
(50) Ayios Nicolaos/Sitia/Ierapetra
(51) Rethymno/Hanis
(52) Kastelli/Viannos
(53) Anoyia/Milopotamos
(54) Archanes

VICE-CONSULATES
(55) United Kingdom
     W. Germany
(56) France
(57) Sweden
(58) Holland
(59) Finland
(60) Denmark
(61) Norway

67

Above: The Bembo Fountain at Kornarou Square.

Below: The famous Lions Fountain at Fountain Square.

(17) THE BEMBO FOUNTAIN —
This is close to the other side of the Market and was built in 1588. It has incorporated a headless Roman statue which was brought in from Ierapetra. A small building next to it was once a Turkish Minaret.

(18) AYIOS MINAS CATHEDRAL -
A large and impressive church with very interesting bell towers. It is a fairly modern church built between 1862-1895 when it was inaugurated. It is very close to the oldest and much smaller church of **AYIOS MINAS** (18A) which contains some excellent wood carvings.

Ayios Minas is the patron saint of the city. A legend says that when the Turks were threatening to slaughter Christian citizens of the town, the saint appeared in the sky on a horse and scared off the oppressors thus saving the people.

(4) ST. KATHERINE'S — *(see also collections)*. To the west side of the square where Ayios Minas Cathedral is, this small Venetian style church contains an excellent collection of Cretan Renaissance icons and paintings.

(19) ST. PETER'S — Situated opposite Xenia Hotel this Venetian church belonged to the Dominican Order and was built around the 15th century. It became a mosque under the Turks and fell into disuse afterwards. Restoration work started in the early 1970's and it is hopeful that it will be completed soon.

(20) PANAYIA STAVROFOROS —
(Our Lady of the Cross Bearer) Originally this was a Venetian Catholic Church of **Santa Maria dei Crosiferi.** The interior is of a true Byzantine style and contains some excellent old paintings and icons.

Above: Detail of Ayios Titos Church. *Below:* The Cathedral of Ayios Minas with the original church to the left of the picture.

69

0 100 200 300 400 500M

MAKARIOU
SOFOKLEIS VENIZELO
SKORDHILON
KAZANTZAKIS

KAMINIA
(Karaoli)

MAKHI
ISKHILIS
SOONV
GORTINA

62

62 MARTIRON
KALOKERINOU

ANOYIA

DION FRANGIADHA

NEO STADIO
(Broumis)

63

MINOOS
THENON

MATALON
MINOOS

TO RETHYMNO/HANIA/
FESTOS/MATALA/HOTELS

LEVINOS
SFAKIDON

KONDHILAKI
VASSIPSILAKI

KYKLADON
YIANNI

SOROVOLOU

PLATIA
NIKEAS

TASIL SBOKOU

PINIKOU
PATRIARII FOTIOU

ASTABAS

W. PLASTIRA
PYRANTHIOU

N.PLASTIRA

VIKELA

EPTANISSOU

AKADIMIAS

VAS

NEAS IOANIAS

SVOKO

AKADIMIA

G. PAP

KASSO

2

21

13

3

18

16

8

29

10

The Vegetable Market.

(1) Museum
(2) Historical Museum
(3) St. Mark
(5) Venetian Harbour
(6) The Castle
(8) Venetian Walls
(10) Kazantzakis Tomb
(11) Ayios Titos
(12) Loggia
(13) Fountain Square
(15) Eleftherias Square
(16) The Market
(18) Ayios Minas
     Cathedral

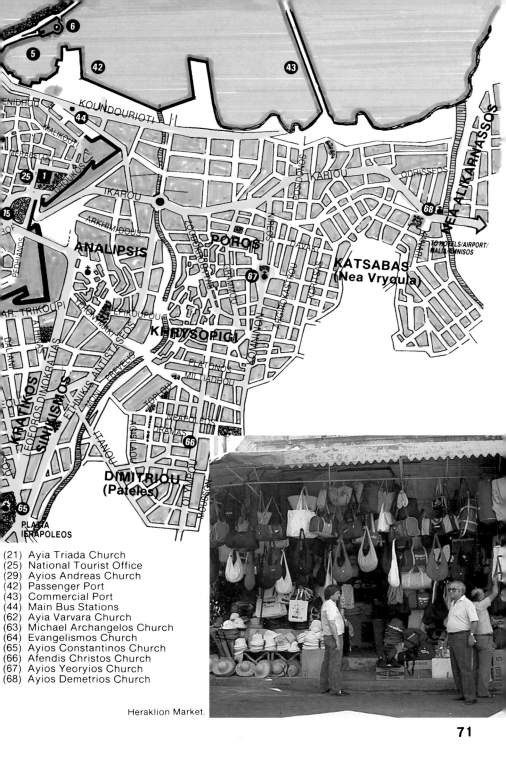

(21) Ayia Triada Church
(25) National Tourist Office
(29) Ayios Andreas Church
(42) Passenger Port
(43) Commercial Port
(44) Main Bus Stations
(62) Ayia Varvara Church
(63) Michael Archangelos Church
(64) Evangelismos Church
(65) Ayios Constantinos Church
(66) Afendis Christos Church
(67) Ayios Yeoryios Church
(68) Ayios Demetrios Church

Heraklion Market.

Above: The Venetian Castle in the harbour.
Below: A scene from Platia (Square) Kornarou, close to the old market

In all, Heraklion is a large bustling city that lovers of history will cherish. There are two harbours, the outer one being modern and immense. Overlooking and dominating the smaller inner harbour is a fine Venetian Castle, originally built by the Arabs in the 9th century. The Venetians who later occupied Crete, also left their mark on Heraklion. The old part of the city is encircled by a fortified wall which in places is 60 feet thick. The wall is pierced by a number of gates through which the road and a steady stream of traffic flows.

Heraklion also boasts a fine museum with fascinating Minoan treasures on display that cannot be seen anywhere else in the world. Just south of Heraklion is another huge tourist pull, the Minoan Palace of Knossos *(both the museum and Knossos are described fully).*

Heraklion, is not only a historians paradise — it is also one for shoppers and gourmets. Come evening, Heraklion abounds in discos, cinemas and live music establishments. There is certainly an endless choice ideal for all pockets Heraklion in fact, has become a cosmopolitan city, yet it lacks good beaches. However, take a bus or hire a taxi and within 15 minutes you can lay and relax on a fair number of excellent beaches — most providing good facilities.

PUBLIC TRANSPORT
KTEL 282 697

Both Heraklion town and the district are covered with an excellent public transport network.

(A) HERAKLION & ENVIRONS also nearby beaches

BUS No. 1 — EAST: Poros—Alikarnassos — Stratones — AIRPORT — Karteros — EOT Beach —Amnisos — Tobruk.
WEST: Hanioporta — Dilino — Yofyro — Ammoudara

BUS No. 2 — HARBOUR — City centre — Ayii Yianni — Venizelos Hospital —KNOSSOS —Spilia — Skalani

BUS No. 3 — HARBOUR — City Centre — Ayii Yianni — Venizelos Hospital —FORTESSA.

BUS No. 4 — MARKET — City Centre — Mustaba.

BUS No. 5 — HARBOUR — City Centre — Dimitriou.

AIR CONNECTIONS
If required, contact OLYMPIC AIRWAYS for timetables, ticket bookings or any flight changes. PLATIA ELEFTHERIAS (LIBERTY SQU-ARE): Tel. 225 171-4 or at Ethnikis Antistaseos Street branch — Tel. 225 171.
Airport: 282 025.

SEA CONNECTIONS
Regular Services to Pireaus.
MINOAN LINES: — 7 Kallergon Square. Tel. 224 304.
ANEK LINES — 33, 25th August Street, Tel. 222 481

Heraklion-Santorini Services, between June and September
KROUSTANOS TOURS: 21, 25th August Street, Tel. 280 048
PALEOLOGOU TOURS 3, 25th August Street, Tel. 283 086

HERAKLION FESTIVAL
The municipality of Heraklion organises every year a summer festival from June to September which includes exhibitions, Crafts & Arts, Folklore, Theatrical Plays and overseas cultural visits of orchestras, music groups, dancing and singing groups etc. For further information and a programme you may apply **Press & Public Relations Officer** — Heraklion Summer Festival Municipality of Heraklion — Tel. 282221.

ENTERTAINMENT
Heraklion town is the centre of Cretan enter-tainment with excellent restaurants specialising in Cretan food. Some also provide a selection of international dishes. Night life including Bou-zouki clubs, Cretan clubs and discotheques are numerous and together with the cinemas and night clubs, provide entertainment for everyone. Entertainment including good eating places, discotheques and Greek entertainment are also to be found at most tourist centres such as Hersonissos, Malia etc.

Amongst the well known high spots with Greek music and dancing are KASTRO near the Arch. Museum, ARETOUSA, on the road to Knossos, PSILORITIS at Rafineria Talos and NTE-LINA which also operates during winter.

USEFUL ADDRESSES — HERAKLION CODE (081)

NATIONAL TOURIST OFFICE (EOT) Platia Eleftherias (Opposite Museum)	Tel: 222 487/8
TOURIST POLICE—Leoforos Dikeosinis	283 190
POST OFFICE—Platia Daskaloyianni (Square)	282 764
OTE (Telephones & Telegrams) Mivotavrou St., (behind El-Greco Park)	282 299
Archaeological Museum—Platia Eleftherias (Square)	282 305
Historical Museum — Bedenaki Street	283 219
ELPA (Automobile Association) El-Greco Park	289 440
General Hospital — Kamaraki Street	282 390
Venizelos Hospital — Knossos Road	289 181
Passport Office	282 379
Police	283 190
Harbour Authorities	282 002
EMERGENCIES	100
SPORTS: Tennis Club	283 015
Mountaineering	287 110
Hunting Club	288 272
Nautical Club	221 128
Munincipality	282 142
Hospital	231 932
First Aids Station	222 222
Banks: Bank of Crete	224 383
Bank of Greece	282 330
National Bank	282 236
Commercial Bank	225 531
Credit Bank	222 443
Ionian & Popular	221 742
General Bank	223 760

ARCHAEOLOGICAL SITES

Heraklion District is full of ancient Minoan Palaces, and archaeological sites, in fact, the richest region of Crete. Below we describe all the interesting sites starting with the best known sites.

KNOSSOS

Probably the most revered name in Crete and the place that nearly all visitors to the island wish to visit and explore. The site can be reached easily from Heraklion. If, of course, you are part of an organised coach tour, you have no problems except keeping up with the time and following the rest of your group. But if you require more time of your own, there are two easy ways to get there. Either by hiring a car and it is only a short drive from Heraklion town and at Knossos you will find parking space *(more traffic is about in the height of the season so be warned)*, or best of all ways, by bus. There are regular bus services at the peak of the season every 15 minutes starting by the main Heraklion Bus station by the harbour.

General opening hours are: April-September 7.30-7pm (Sundays and holidays 10-6), October-March 8.00-Sundown. The site is closed on Christmas Day, New Year, Greek Easter, 25 March, 28 October.

On the way to KNOSSOS you go through **AYIOS IOANNIS** — with excellent views of Heraklion and the Bay. Here was a remarkable

domed Tomb of the Middle Minoan period, unfortunately it was destroyed during the German occupation.

THE HOSPITAL (8) on the left hand side as you go towards Knossos, built after the war by Greek Americans, commands exciting views of the valley of Kairatos. While the building was in progress a lot of Minoan tombs were discovered. Further tombs were found in the area dating from the Post Minoan to Roman Periods.

ROMAN VILLA (9) — Easily seen on the right hand side of the road, is a red-roofed structure, under which is protected the mosaic floor of the villa of Dionysos. No road goes there, so you park along the road and go through the fence into the field. The villa was part of a Roman settlement.

VILLA ARIADNE — Further to the south, was built by Sir Arthur Evans where he stayed while exploring Knossos. It was used during the war as the residence of the German Commandant. Now it houses the Greek Archaeological Service.

— Knossos Palace is 5kms to the southeast of Heraklion.

The Restored West Bastion. A copy of the fresco of the Bull in an olive grove is on the wall.

THE HISTORY OF THE PALACE

The present Palace is the remnant of the great Palace of the Neo-Palatial Period 1700-1400BC and it incorporated the remains of earlier and later buildings. In fact, Knossos was settled around 6000BC and contains a very rich accummulation of debris from the Neolithic period. Habitation continued all through the Bronze age and into the early Minoan age.

The first Palace was thought to have been erected in the Middle Minoan period c1950-900BC. It was believed to have been destroyed around 1700BC, perhaps from an earthquake. The Palace was then rebuilt on an enlarged scale. Though damaged between c1600-1580BC it was restored and rebuilt. The structure in various storeys was massive occupying some 20,000 square metres. The **Royal Apartments** also incorporated various workshops and magazines (storerooms) for the produce of the Palace. The **West Wing** was dedicated to the cult of the Goddess. In 1450BC, like all other palaces and Minoan settlements, Knossos suffered an abrupt destruction *(see historical survey).*

Contrary to the fate of other Palaces, Knossos was rebuilt and restored and continued its functions up to c1400BC. However, many archaeologists believe that it was now under the control of the mainland Greeks, the **Myceneans** and during this period it was destroyed again c1400-1380BC in a great conflagration from which it never recovered.

Around the year 1200BC there was some occupation, mainly of the little Palace and the Shrine of the **Double Axes** but after that the Palace was never again occupied. However, the surrounding area was habitated by various people as will be described below.

THE EXCAVATIONS

Although many finds were discovered by local people in and around the Palace in the 19th century, the land was believed to be owned by Turks, thus both the Turkish administration and the owners made it difficult to proceed with any work. An amateur Cretan Archaeologist **Minos Kalokairinos** dug in 1878 around Knossos and discovered massive structures and large storage urns, however the Turkish authorities put a stop to the work. In 1886 Heinrich Schliemann having heard the accounts of this came to Crete but was unsuccessful in his bid to purchase the land.

SIR ARTHUR EVANS, the British archaeologist also came to Crete in 1894 in search of the Palace and after several attempts he managed to purchase all the land in and around the Palace. Excavations began by Evans in 1900. Week after week, careful excavations revealed how massive the place was and after two years continous work, this labyrinthine Palace came to light. With the studies of the excavations, Evans thought it best to reconstruct parts of the Palace and work was careful and complex. By using existing stones and reinforced concrete, re-built considerable parts of the Palace including stairways, walls, columns, it took Evans and his staff of archaeologists, artists and architects many years to finish their work and some restoration still takes place from time to time. However, other scholars disputed the wisdom of the reconstruction and cast doubts on many of Evan's archaeological reports including chronology etc. To most people, the work of Evans has produced a much better understanding and feeling of this ancient Great Wonder.

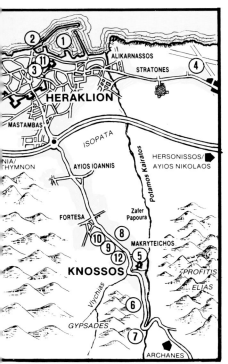

LOCATION MAP OF HERAKLION/KNOSSOS

(1) THE HARBOUR
(2) THE CASTLE
(3) MUSEUM OF HERAKLION
(4) INTERNATIONAL AIRPORT
(5) THE PALACE OF KNOSSOS
(6) ROYAL TEMPLE
(7) MEDIEVAL BRIDGE
(8) ROMAN BASILICA
(9) VILLA DIONYSOS
(10) ROMAN AMPHITHEATRE
(11) BUS STOPS TO KNOSSOS
(12) VILLA ARIADNE

And Wonder it was, with its drainage and sanitation systems, which match our modern 20th century living conditions, it is quite amazing as is the **hydraulic** technology of the East Bastion.

There were no defences around the huge Palace. It was not only the Residence of the Minoan Kings but also contained residential apartments for nobles, functionaries and craftsmen. It also served as a religious centre with chapels and shrines everywhere.

Most of the fascinating works of art including the surviving frescoes were removed to Heraklion Museum and what you admire here are mainly reconstructions. Many of the gigantic PITHOI, some 2 metres high and 4-5 metres in girth are on display here.

The interior lighting problem was also solved. The Minoans thought of a fascinating scheme, Courts and shafts remained open, so the light could get through the various storeys into the lower quarters. Remarkable also were the stairways some being narrow and some grand and wide.

A four-five storey structure, in reality, the palace was **The House of the Doub[le] Axe,** not the *"Labyrinth"* as it was original[ly] *translated from the word* **Labrys** *meanin[g] "double Axe".* Although in the Greek world Mythology, Knossos was associated with as the *Labyrinth.*

"The MINOS Kings, Masters of the Se[a] forced the weak Athenians and oth[er] subject people to contribute, by sending eve[ry] Nine years, Seven Young Men and Seve[n] Young Maidens to be given to the **Minotau[r]** the monstrous son of *Queen Pasiphae* and th[e] *Bull* sent to Minos by Poseidon.

When *Theseus,* the son of the Athenian Kin[g] came as one of the seven young men he fell i[n] love on first sight with Mino's daughte[r] **Ariadne.** She supplied him with a thread f[or] him to find his way out easily, so he entered th[e] labyrinth and in the struggle he killed th[e] Minotaur, thus freeing the Athenians and othe[r] of this terrible monster . . . "

The South Propyleon with reproduced wall painting[s] of the Cup-Bearers.

explore the site with its many rooms and corridors, it is difficult for us or any one else, to provide an exact ~te as to which is the best way to proceed, so it is better that you use your own judgement. Our illustrated ~ns will allow you to position yourself and follow the most suitable direction.

) WEST & SOUTH WEST SIDE

(1) — **Sir Evans** Bronze Bust, as you come from the main entrance.

(2) — **Wall Pits** — original functions unknown, the later Minoans used them as rubbish tip.

(5) — **West Porch** — A base of the single column to be seen, originally the walls were decorated with frescoes.

(6) — **Corridor of the Procession** — once was lined with frescoes.

(9) — **Great Propyleum** — on the southern wing of the Palace with restored doorways and walls around it — see the sacred Horn and frescoes.

(10) — **South Entrance** — once connected to the road which lead to the south and Festos.

(11) — **Corridor of the Priest King** — or *Lily Prince* with a copy of the Prince fresco with lilies, perhaps a priest king.

(12) — **Open Staircase,** leading to the Upper Floor *(Piano Nobile)* — see separate diagram.

) UPPER FLOOR - PIANO NOBILE

(68) — **Great Hall** — with bases of two columns to be seen.

(69) — **Sanctuary Hall,** traces of six columns.

(72) — **Reconstructed Rooms** just above the Throne Complex. Reproduced frescoes of originals found at Knossos and now at Heraklion Museum.

) GROUND FLOOR - WEST WING

(13) — **Magazines with Pithoi** — Store Rooms. These can be seen better from above (Piano Nobile). The chambers of storerooms were closed and no daylight could reach them. Many of the pithoi held wine and oil.

(16 & 19) — Areas where **Linear B tablets** and **Minoan Hieroglyphic** deposits were found. Visible through metal grills are below rooms of the Old Palace.

(17) — **Lustral Area** — Reconstructed, was used for purification bathing containing the deepest lustral basins.

) THEATRICAL AREA

(61) — **Theatre Area** — with stairs on the southern and eastern sides, believed to have been used for ceremonies, dancing etc.

(62) — **Royal Road** *"the Oldest Road in Europe"* which used to join the road to the **Little Palace** excavated in the 1960's.

) NORTH QUARTER

(58) — **Pillar Hall** also known as "Customs House" with its large square pillars.

(56) — **Ramp, bastions** and Colinnaded **Porticos,** some reconstructed. On the second storey of the Portico there are reproductions of Bull frescoes found here.

(57) — **North Entrance,** with the north pillar hall. Reconstruction of a Bull in an olive grove.

) CENTRAL COURT & SURROUNDING AREA

(28) — **CENTRAL COURT** — The dominant part of the Palace, 55 x 28 metres and under it lies the original Neolithic site.

The Central Court was planned unevenly toward the 4 points of the compass with the West and East wings as the main units. All movements to sectors of the Palace started and finished here. Some believe that the Minoan bull games used to take place in the Central Court.

the West of ~ Central ~urt.

(20) — **Throne Room** — Enter through the antechamber (21); the throne in the anteroom is a wooden reproduction. This is the oldest Royal Throne in the world and is made of gypsum. The throne is in the room which is full of wall paintings, mainly floral, all reproductions — the throne room is closed to the public for protection.

(25) — **Lobby of the Stone Seat** — a small open court.

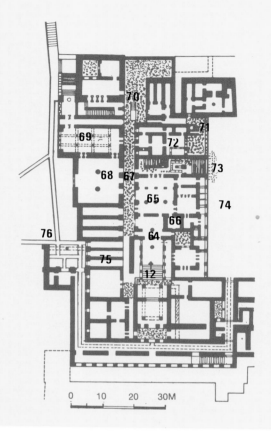

0   10   20   30M

KNOSSOS–Piano Nobile (Upper Floor on West Wing)

(12) Stairs from Grand Propyleum (see also main plan)
(64) Lobby
(65) Tricolumnar Shrine
(66) Temple Treasury
(67) Corridor
(68) Great Hall
(69) Sanctuary Hall
(70) Stairs to Corridors of Magazines
(71) Small staircase reaching Throne Complex
(72) Reconstructed Terrace & Rooms
(73) Staircase down to Central Hall
(74) also (28) Central Hall
(75) Magazines
(76) West Court

KNOSSOS PALAC

MAIN FLOOR (See page 79)

(1) Sir Arthur Evans Bust
(2) Walled Pits
(3) West Court
(4) Altar
(5) West Porch
(6) Corridor of the Procession
(7) South House
(8) South Corridor
(9) Great Propyleum (South)
(10) South Entrance
(11) Corridor of the Priest King (Lilly Prince)
(12) Staircase to Piano Nobile (see Upper Floor plan)
(13) Magazines with Pithoi
(14) Corridor of the Magazines
(15) Stairs from Piano Nobile

0 10 20 30 40 50M

(23) — **Room of the large Pithos** — A tall Pithos.

(22) — **Temple Repositories** — Storage of treasures and offerings to the shrine. one of the crypts was found the **Snake Goddess** *(Heraklion Museum).*

(24) — **Pillar Crypts** — 2 rooms with pillars — in the centre, of some sacre character crypts — with signs of double axes.

(27) — **Site of Greek Temple** — the only late structure found in the Palace.

To the East of the Central Court

(29) — **Grand Staircase** — one of the major architectural achievements of antiquit now protected, leading to a hall.

(32) — **Hall of the Colonnades** — from the Grand Staircase, with its typical ligl shaft to the right.

(33) — **King's Room** — with the restored room of the "Double Axes" with a repli of the king's wooden throne; it is believed that the king held court here.

(34) — **Queen's Megaron** — Reconstructed hall with floral decorations an reproduced Dolphin frescoes.

(37) — **Queen's Toilet Room** — with remains of the **Flush Toilet** and other signs the drainage system.

(36) **Treasury** — where many inscribed tablets were found.

(G) NORTH EAST SIDE and Palace Wing-Workshops

(46) — **Eastern Portico** — leading to Patter's Workshops (47) with benches an receptacles, also known as the "schoolroom".

(50) — **Grand Pithoi** — enclosed magazines.

(49) — **Eastern Bastion** — stairs leading down — reconstruction ha taken place — Evans suggested that the loundry was here.

(53) — **Corridor of the Draughtsboard,** named after a gameboard found here now at Heraklion Museum, *Case 57.* Drain pipes survive from the firs palace.

(51) — **Royal Pottery** — Store room.

(31) — **Metallion Pithoi** — Narrow magazines with giant jars, still here, s named from their decorations.

(30) — **Corridor of the Bays** — massive piers probably supporting the grea East hall on which was believed stood a giant statue of a Minoan Goddess

(H) SOUTH EAST WING

(38) — **Bathroom** — a small room with a bath tub.

(39) — **Room of Jars** — another small room with 3 jars.

(40) — **Shrine of Double Axes** — a small enclosed shrine, built after th destruction of the great palace.

The Queen's Hall
as being restored.

Above: The Anteroom of the Throne Room with a wooden replica of the throne. *Below:* A reproduction of the Bull-Leaping Fresco — the original is at Heraklion Museum.

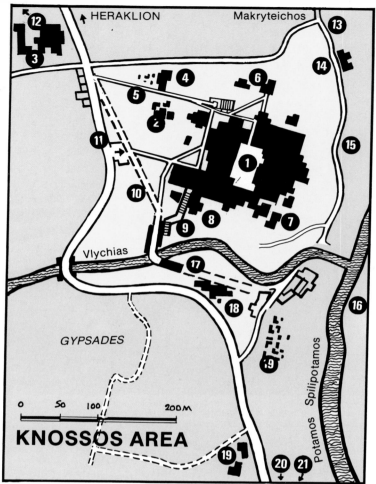

KNOSSOS AREA

(1) THE PALACE
(2) House of Frescoes
(3) Little Palace
(4) Armoury or Arsenal
(5) Royal Road
(6) North Pillar House
(7) South East House
(8) South House
(9) Stepped Portio
(10) Ancient Road (Ruins)
(11) Cafes
(11) Main Entrance/Car Park
(12) Villa Ariadne
(13) Roman Antiquities
(14) Royal Villa
(15) Arena
(16) Minoan Cemeteries
(17) Minoan Viaduct
(18) Guests Houses
     (Caravenserai)
(19) Minoan Houses
(20) To House of High Priest
(21) To Royal Temple
     & Tomb

THE AREA AROUND THE PALACE

Knossos was not only a Palace but a whole city believed to have reached, at the peak of the Minoan period, over 50,000 inhabitants. Serious students of archaeology can enjoy exploring the area around searching for tombs, stones and shrines. Most of the important places including the **Royal Villa,** the **Little Palace** and the **Temple Tomb** are closed to the public and special permission is needed.

(2) THE HOUSE OF FRESCOES —

Is located to the south of the Royal Road. A small house, with a good floor on the south east corner. An interesting place for it was here that many fine frescoes (wall paintings) were found. They show the Royal Gardens, Blue Bird, Blue Monkey and the leader of the Blacks.

LOCATION MAP OF KNOSSOS AREA

(1) THE PALACE
(2) House of Frescoes
(3) Little Palace
(4) Armouri or Arsenal
(5) Royal Road
(6) North Pillar House
(9) Stepped Portio
(10) Ancient Road
(11) Entrance/Parking
(12) Villa Ariadne
(13) Roman Antiquities
(14) Roman Villa
(15) Arena
(16) Minoan Cemeteries
(17) Minoan Viaduct
(18) Guest Houses
(19) Minoan Houses
(20) House of High Priest
(21) Royal Temple/Tomb
(22) Roman Ruins

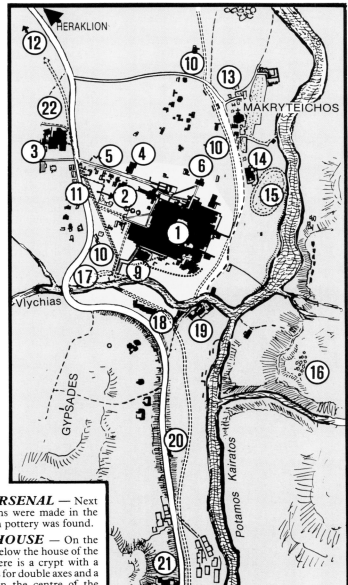

(4) ARMOURY or ARSENAL — Next to it further excavations were made in the late 1950's and Minoan pottery was found.

(7) SOUTH EAST HOUSE — On the south east side, it lies below the house of the **Chancel Screen.** There is a crypt with a single pillar, two stands for double axes and a tall porphyry lamp. In the centre of the house there is a rectangular room, three of its walls built of ashlar limestone blocks.

(8) SOUTH HOUSE — Built after 1600BC, parts of the floor and two upper storeys survived and partly restored with a third floor.

(14) ROYAL VILLA — 4-5 minutes walk from the East Bastion — on the hillside facing eastwards toward the river. The ground floor survived and part of the first floor has been restored. It was originally a 3 storey building. It contains a main hall, hall, light wells, pillar crypt. The overall layout of the house is unusual and was believed to have had some special significance.

On the landing of the staircase a magnificent Palace style jar with relief papyrus was found — now at Heraklion Museum. The villa was built in the middle Minoan period.

(3) LITTLE PALACE — To the west of the modern road before Knossos, the largest building after the Palace, it consists of a main hall with a crazy paved floor, a series of stately halls on the east and to the west a number of rooms and remains of a staircase. The Lustral area was used as a shrine. Linear B tablets were found here, but the most important find is that of the famous **Bull's Head Rhyton.** It was built in the Middle Minoan period and destroyed at the same time as the main palace.

(18) CARAVANSERAI - GUEST HOUSE — Generally used by guests of the Palace. Two rooms facing the palace have been restored and a reproduction of the famous Partridge Frescoe, found here, has been painted on the walls of the eastern room. The **spring chamber,** has been restored, is near the Guest House. The chamber was full of pottery remains and offerings of the Minoan period and it was used as a shrine.

(17) MINOAN VIADUCT — Massive piers over the stream of Vlychia. Built of huge blocks and between the piers there are 4-5 steps going down to the water level. It was a resting place for travellers from the south.

(20) HOUSE OF HIGH PRIEST — Very little left of the house. A stone-altar was found here set behind a columnar balustrade with stands of double axes on both sides.

(21) ROYAL TEMPLE TOMB — An interesting combination of Tomb and Temple partially restored by Evans. It was built in the Middle Minoan period and was used up to the destruction of the Palace. It was built as a burial place below and a Temple above. A well preserved Minoan monument.

The Temple Tomb to the South of the Palace

FESTOS (PHAISTOS) PALACE

Tel: (0892) 22615

The second most important Minoan Palace in Crete. It was built on the side of a lone hilltop, commanding panoramic views, on three sides, of the MESARA valley. An ideal place to build a palace for its beautiful views and its protected position. A tourist pavilion provides refreshments, snacks and toilets. There are bus connections with Heraklion. Its history goes deep into the Neolithic period and it was established as an important place in the early Minoan period.

The first Palace was built in the Middle Minoan period around 1900BC, then was rebuilt in various periods with additions and reconstructions. The Second Palace was destroyed at the same time as all other palaces c145BC. Later, re-occupation includes the Bronze Age, Geometric, Classical and Hellenistic.

The importance of Festos was parallel to Knossos and there is a similarity in design and structure of the two palaces. Minos Kings, connected Festos and Knossos wih an excellent road system. The people living here were known for their wit. When the palace was excavated it was left more or less in the state in which it was found although some walls were strengthened.

Excavations were started here at the same time as by Evans at Knossos — here by an Italian team headed by **Halbherr** and **Pernier.** It was completed in 1909. However, further excavations continued later on and still continue from time to time, in and around the Palace.

Above: Large Pithoi (jars) by the northern side of the Central Hall.
Below: General view of the Northern side.

85

TOURING THE PALACE

Festos is not as complicated to tour as Knossos, and while exploring the ruins, you can always rest by looking at the surrounding countryside.

(A) THE WEST COURT

(2) — **Upper Court** — Originally Protopalatian, most of today's remains are of houses of later settlers, post Minoan Greeks.

(5) — **Step seats** — Eight long steps (20 metres or longer) with seating capacity of around 500 people, suggesting ceremonial seating in the theatrical area.

(6) **West Court** — The court of the first Palace used for theatrical and other ceremonies, perhaps even religious.

(8) **Walled Pits** — *Koulouras* – the original use of them is disputed although a strong view is that they are silos that held grain.

The Old Palace is along the south-west, most parts of which are closed to visitors for protection. They include **Old Palace Propylon** (16); ramp let up a bastion to the **2nd level** (17), **Old Entrance Palace** (18), **Facade** of the Old Palace (9) — the facade was altered after the reconstruction of the second Palace.

(10) — **GRAND STAIRWAY** — and Entrance. A truly grand staircase approx. 13 metres wide slightly rising in the middle. Some of the stairs are carved out of natural rock. The side walls are of ashlar masonry.

(11) — **Propylon** of new Palace. At the top of the staircase, through two doorways and column bases (3 in all) into a small area.

(B) (25) CENTRAL COURT

To the same measurements as that of Knossos (51 x 22 metres). An impressive court providing panoramic views to the south. It was paved with limestone and some slabs survive. Along the west and east sides were colonnades, some bases survive.

(c) WEST WING

(13) — **Lobby of the Magazines** — a lower storeroom of the old palace with some pithoi still in place.

(12) — **Corridor of the Magazines** – on both sides along the corridor there are storerooms, some still containing some large pithoi, some of the pithoi were storing oil.

(22) — **Rooms with benches,** two small rooms one with a low plaster table in the middle, possibly for offerings from the nearby shrine.

(20) — **Lustral Basin** — Similar to that of Knossos with descending steps and a parapet.

(19) — **Greek Temple of Rhea** — to the far end, south west. This temple was erected after the Minoan civilisation ceased to exist and is right up to the edge of the hill.

The Grand Staircase.

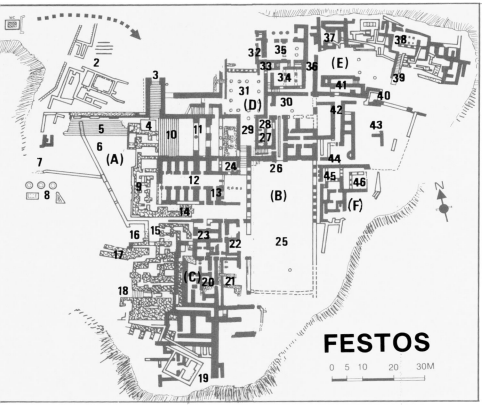

(A) = **West Court**	(21) Room of the Pillars
(B) = **Central Court**	(22) Rooms with benches
(C) = **West Wing**	(23) Shrine of the West Wing
(D) = **North Wing**	(24) Room of Lustral Basin
(E) = **North East Wing**	(25) CENTRAL COURT
(F) = **East Wing**	(26) Entrance to passageway

(A) = **West Court**
(B) = **Central Court**
(C) = **West Wing**
(D) = **North Wing**
(E) = **North East Wing**
(F) = **East Wing**

(1) TOURIST PAVILION
(2) Upper Court
(3) Staircase to West Court
(4) Old Palace Shrine
(5) Step Seats (Tiers of Theatre)
(6) West Court
(7) To Old Palace Remains
(8) Walled Pits
(9) Facade of Old Palace
(10) Grand Stairway
(11) Propylon of New Palace
(12) Corridors & Magazines
(13) Lobby of the Magazines
(14) Kitchen Area
(15) Passage to Central Court
(16) Old Palace
(17) Ramp
(18) Old Palace Entrance
(19) Greek Temple of Rhea
(20) Lustral Basin

(21) Room of the Pillars
(22) Rooms with benches
(23) Shrine of the West Wing
(24) Room of Lustral Basin
(25) CENTRAL COURT
(26) Entrance to passageway
(27) Interior Court
(28) Interior Court
(29) Area Toward Peristyle

(30) Interior Court
(31) Peristyle
(32) Cistern
(33) Stairs
(34) Queen's Megaron
(35) King's Megaron
(36) Corridor
(37) Archive
(38) Peristyle House

(39) Stairs
(40) Guard Room
(41) Lustral Basin
(42) Corridor toward East Court
(43) Metal or Pottery Furnace
(44) Corridor
(45) Prince's Suite
(46) Collonade

The Corridor of the Magazines.

87

(D) NORTH WING

(26) — **Central Doorway** — with bases for columns (probably wooden) and into a corridor with various rooms on each side.

(27 & 28) — **Interior Courts** which had small cupboards on the walls.

(30) — **North Court** — walled court with a round cistern in the centre.

(34) — **Queens Court** — now covered for protection and partly restored. The court had four columns in the middle which indicates an open area around the rooms.

(31) — **Peristyle Hall** — second storey was reached by a stairway (33). Must have been an impressive area.

(35) — **Kings Rooms** — A two room complex with a light well. On the north side it commanded panoramic views of Messara valley and the Idi mountains in the background. There are signs of frescoes on the lower parts of walls and are protected with a cover.

(E) NORTH EAST WING

(37) — **Archives,** mainly used as a storage place of ritual objects. Linear A tablets were found here but the most important find was the famous **Festos Disc** now at Heraklion Museum *case 41* room 111.

(38) — **Peristyle House** — an open central space with pillars and columns perhaps a private house.

(F) EAST WING

(41) — **Lustral basin** — a lustral bath.

(40) — **Guard Room** — Guarding the entry into the Palace from the east.

(43) — **Metal or Pottery Furnace** — There are the remains of a kiln here and it is believed to be the workshops and living quarters of craftsmen.

(46) — **Collonade** — bases of columns are to be seen.

(45) — **Prince's Suite** — This was designated to the Prince of the Palace.

It is interesting to note that the Palace of Festos, like all other Minoan Palaces was not fortified.

Other remains of interest, mainly to archaeologists are found around the Palace on hill slopes and include graves and houses.

AYIA TRIADA

This site is situated to the west of Festos and close to the sea in a place called *"Paradise"*, full of fruit trees and not far from the Greek Airforce Base.

The site was either a large villa, a summer palace, or a prince's residence. No name has survived from the Minoan period, so the name of Ayia Triada was given from the village which once existed there. The only surviving element of the old village is the chapel of **Ayios Yeoryios Galatas,** 15th century (21).

The Minoan buildings have the usual chambers, courtyards, terraces and storage vaults but not a central court, a main feature of all Minoan Palaces, thus suggesting that it was used by the rulers of Festos as a residence of pleasure. The most significant remains are the two circular stone-built **tholos tombs.**

Around the area, many Minoan tombs were excavated and amongst the finds is a **painted sarcofagus,** now in room XIV at Heraklion Museum and some tablets of Linear A inscriptions.

Although Ayia Triada is not as spectacular as Knossos or Festos, it is however an important Minoan site.

SHORT DESCRIPTION

(3) **Minoan Road** — This was the main road leading to the Palace of Festos.

A General View of Ayia Triada.

(4) Storerooms — This is the east wing with storerooms. Also here are remains of a large late Minoan House where a fine bronze Double Axe was found.

(7) Ramb-stairs — This is along the north side of the building leading to the northwest side.

(8) Central Corridor — which leads to the north east sector, going through the Mycenean Megaron (12) on both sides.

(11) Small treasury — here were found 19 bronze "talents" now at Heraklion Museum.

(13) Queen's Hall — Here some frescoes were found and are on display at Heraklion Museum.

(14) Archives Room — A deposit of clay sealings used for sealstones were found here.

(16) Rooms of Mosaics — Very exquisite mosaics were found here including a seated lady in a garden and a cat stalking a pheasant, now at Heraklion Museum.

(17) Terrace Area — on the side of a cliff, provides fine views of the area and the mountains of Idi.

(18) Men's Hall — a colonnaded hall, the main room of the villas, some 6 x 9 metres leading to the terrace *(above)*.

(20) Storage rooms — Main western storage area with magazines, and also servant's quarters. From one room came the well known *"serpentine relief cup"* with a captain and a band of soldiers.

(21) Ayios Yeoryios Galatas — A Venetian Chapel with some remains of frescoes.

(23) Late Minoan stairs, leading into the Late Minoan Agora (25) and the Late Minoan settlement to the west (24)

(26) Magazines or shops on the eastern side of the late Minoan Town Houses and the Agora, are the magazines or shops, buildings unique of their type in Minoan architecture.

(27) Town Area — with remains of houses of the Late Minoan period 14 to 13th century BC.

(28) To Tombs — The whole cemetery is easily accessible to the north east of the settlement and includes the two circular tombs.

AYIA TRIADA

(1) Entrance from Festos New Road
(2) Caretaker's Pavilion
(3) Minoan Road
(4) Storerooms
(5) South Court
(6) Drainage System
(7) Ramp-Stairs
(8) Central Corridor
(9) Room with Column
(10) Facade of Villa
(11) Small Treasury
(12) Mycenaean Megaron
(13) Queen's Hall
(14) Archives Room
(15) Portico
(16) Room of Mosaics
(17) Terrace Area
(18) Mevis Hall
(19) Old Paved Road
(20) Store rooms and servant's quarters
(21) Ayios Yeoryios Galatas Church

(22) Middle Minoan House
(23) Late Minoan Stairs
(24) Remains of Late Minoan Settlement
(25) Late Minoan Agora
(26) Magazines or Shops
(27) Town Area
(28) To Tombs

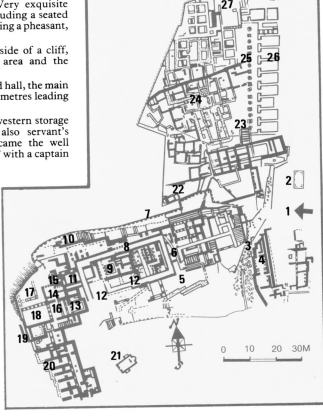

GORTYNA (GORTYS)

A very important archaeological site, in fact the most important Non-Minoan site of ancient Crete. It was believed to have been established by the DORIANS after the Minoan civilization ended. By the 8th century BC it was a commercial centre and was using as its ports, **Matala** *(to the west)* and **Leben** *(to the south)*.

Between the 8 and 5th centuries BC it had become a very advanced society with its own laws *(see historical section and below)*. As an established and strong power it was continuously engaging in wars with other Cretan cities. It is also said that Hannibal came here in 189BC.

With the Roman occupation of Crete, Gortyna became a perfect provincial city and enjoyed a long period of prosperity and expansion due to the surrounding rich agricultural land. In fact, Gortys became the Roman Capital of Crete and Cyrenaica.

It continued flourishing under the early Christian period when a large Cathedral was built. However, decline followed in later years and eventually it was destroyed by the Arabs. The ancient city is spread over a wide area amongst olive groves on both sides of the main road, but most of the remains are of the Roman period.

Descriptions of the most important places are as numbered in the map.

(1) AYIOS TITOS BASILICA — Situated
to the north side of the main road close to the parking area, is mainly in ruins with only one part remaining of this once very spectacular church. On the northern side there is still a chapel in use as a shrine, containing some original frescoes.

Ayios Titos Basilica — A General View.

The Basilica was built by the first bishop of Gortyna — **TITUS** who was asked personally by St. Paul to erect a very impressive and huge basilica in order to impress the local pagan people. However, the existing basilica dates to the 6th century.

(2) ODEON & LAW CODES — The
Roman Odeon was built over an existing Hellenistic one. It was rebuilt by Emperor Trajan in 100AD and incorporates a building of the 1st century BC. Behind the small reconstructed ODEON are the famous **LAW CODES OF GORTYNA** sheltered under a modern brick built gallery.

The Law Codes were carved on stone blocks by the Dorian Cretans around 450BC and were publicly displayed to the people, unfortunately, many of them were destroyed by the Romans who used the blocks for other purposes.

For those that survived, more than 70,000 characters have been counted, carved mainly in Greek characters and nearly 18 letters of the ancient Greek alphabet have been recognised. The script was set down in what is called an *OX PLOUGH* manner. What it really means is that you read one line across from left to right, then the following line from right to left, then left to right, right to left and so on.

These codes are mainly amendments of much more ancient Laws and they deal essentially with civil matters such as marriage, divorce, adultery, property, rights of citizens, adoption, mortgages and other aspects of daily life.

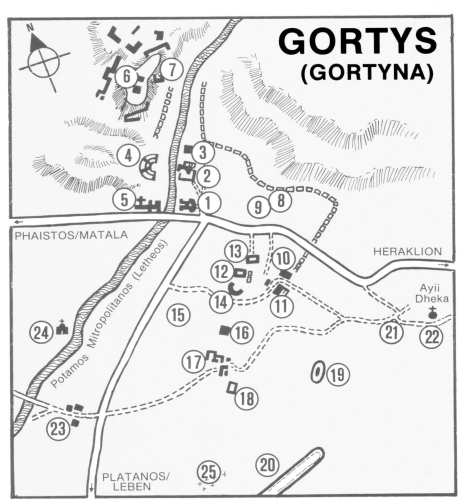

GORTYS
(GORTYNA)

N

PHAISTOS/MATALA

HERAKLION

Potamos Mitropolitanos (Letheos)

Ayii
Dheka

PLATANOS/
LEBEN

(1) AYIOS TITOS BASILICA
(2) ODEON & LAW CODES
(3) The Mill
(4) Hellenistic Theatre
(5) Storage Chambers
(6) The Acropolis
(7) The Altar
(8) Aqueduct
(9) Tourist Pavillion (Inactive?)
10) The Nymphaeum
11) Praetorium
12) Temple of Pythian Apollo
13) Sanctuary of Isis & Therapis
14) The Theatre
15) Byzantine Basilica
16) Nymphaion
17) Baths
18) Main Gate
19) Amphitheatre

(20) The Stadium
(21) Local Museum
(22) Chapel of Ayii Dheka

(23) Metropolis
(24) Early Christian Basilica
(25) Cemetery Area

Gortys Ruins
and the Temple of
Pythian Apollo
in the background.

(3) THE MILL — This abandoned mill is of the Venetian period and was used until quite recently for grinding flour.

(4) HELLENISTIC THEATRE — Opposite the Odeon, over the other side of the valley of the river, it is mainly in ruins, though now partly restored.

(5) STORAGE CHAMBERS — These are situated on both sides of the main road, but mainly on the northern side, west of the Basilica and are now in ruins.

(6) THE ACROPOLIS — Overlooking the site from the northwest side the Acropolis was inhabited in many different periods including Neolithic, Late Minoan, Sub-Minoan and Bronze Ages.

The remains of the **TEMPLE** are of the Geometric to Archaic periods 8 to 7th centuries BC and innside there was a stonecult statue of 3 naked female figures, now on display at Heraklion Museum. Homer's Illiad states that the city was walled.

Around the slopes of the Acropolis various remains of the Hellenistic and Roman periods were uncovered and also an **Altar** (7) of the Archaic period — a place of sacrifice, and many terracotta figures and other religious objects were found around it.

The Ruins of the Odeon and the building which houses the famous Law Codes.

(10) THE NYMPHAEUM — Built around the 2nd century AD it became a public fountain during the Christian period

(11) PRAETORIUM — The residence of the Roman Governor of the Province.

(12) TEMPLE OF PYTHIAN APOLLO — This was the main sanctuary of the city and the original dates to the Archaic era and was built on the site of an earlier Minoan building. Additions followed in the Hellenistic period. Further Roman additions and modifications occured.

(13) SANCTUARY OF ISIS & SERAPIS — This rectangular cellar with its annexes was Roman built by Flavia Phyilyra and her family.

(14) THEATRE — Remains of the brick-built Roman theatre exist and can be seen.

(18) MAIN GATE — Only the remains of a vast Roman structure are evident.

(19) AMPHITHEATRE — Roman origin, dating from the 2nd cent. AD.

(20) THE STADIUM — Only traces of what was once the stadium of the city, remain.

(21) THE MUSEUM — A new building completed in 1979 and houses various items found on the site including inscriptions, sculptures etc.

ARKHANES

This important ancient site, close to the town of Arkhanes was a late discovery. Real digging started in 1964 and has produced some remarkable and valuable finds. Excavations are continuing and although enough excitement has been generated, their true rewards are yet to be assessed.

(1) FOURNI CEMETERY. This is to the north western side of Arkhanes town, the richest and most extensive cemetery in the entire Prehistoric Aegean area. Structures and Tombs date from 2500 to 1250BC. There are three well preserved **Tholos Tombs** c1400BC. The finds were enormous and rich, including about 140 pieces of excellent jewellery, ceramics, cycladic white marble, female idols and obidian objects, thus indicating extensive habitation of the area.

Also found here was the first intact **Royal Burial Complex** of Minoan Crete with a sarcophagus containing a woman: a royal, a priestess or a wealthy woman with over 140 pieces of various items including gold jewellery, pottery, bronze vessels, ivory pieces and necklaces.

Many of the cemetery's finds are at Heraklion Museum.

(2) THE PALACE or a very large **Villa**, as some archaeologists believe, was a well constructed Minoan building dating to around 1600BC. Floral frescoes found here are now at Heraklion Museum. Some of the surviving walls have heights of up to 3 metres.

(3) ANEMOSPILIA TEMPLE (Anemospilia = Cave of the Wind). No spectacular remains exist here but the views of the surrounding area from the hill top are so beautiful that a visitor to Arkhanes should not miss this spot. It is situated about 4kms to the northwest of the town.

ARKHANES
Map not in scale

(1) Fourni Cemetery
(2) Minoan Palace
(3) Anemospilia Temple
(4) Chapel
(5) Church
(6) School
(7) Small Bridge

The **Temple** was a sacred place a presumed cult and offerings were found. Also, an extraordinary find of human skeletons (i) a **female** — face down, (ii) a **male** — suggested from his jewellery that he was a priest and (iii) a third — a **young man** — lying in a foetal position on his side on what appears to be an altar, with a long 40cm bronze knife lying on the skeleton.

The latter, specially, suggested the explanation to scholars that a human sacrifice had been performed, when the building collapsed, perhaps due to an earthquake.

TYLISSOS

This site is situated to the outskirts of the modern village of Tylissos. This Minoan site comprises three large villas and a post Minoan Megaron. Most of the remains date to c1600-1450BC.

Further construction was carried out in the Post-Minoan period, and under the Dorians, it was an important city with its own mint. The Dorians also worshipped here the *Goddess Artemis*. Many of the finds include Linear A tablets, (are on display at Heraklion Museum). They also include storage jars, a fine bronze statuette and miniature frescoes in pieces.

(A) – HOUSE-I – This is the middle of the complex. It contains 2 large **magazines** (5) and big storage jars, pillar base indicating that pillars were supporting an upper storey. Further **magazines** are on the southern part of the house (8 & 9) and in one of them, gigantic bronze cauldrous and linear A tablets were found.

(B) – HOUSE-II – To the southwest side, a smaller and less well preserved complex. The house was built over an earlier foundation *(Pre-Minoan)*. A staircase on the north-eastern side led to the upper floor.

93

(C) - HOUSE-III - This house is on the northern side and some good paving has survived in the eastern rooms. The magazines are situated on the western side of the **house** (14) and in one room there is a column from the late Minoan III period.

The northern corridor has remains of various periods including later Greek buildings. Some of the walls are well preserved. In the north side there is a **large hall** with two columns (19) and an **open court** to the west side (23). To the eastern side there is a circular **cistern** (24) from where water was carried by a stone channel.

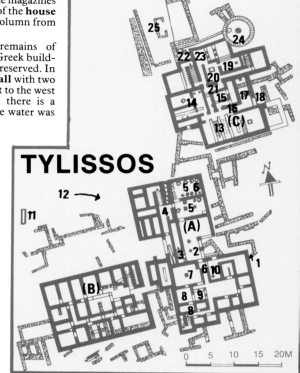

TYLISSOS

(A) = HOUSE I

(1) Entrance
(2) Entrance
(3) Stairs to Upper Floor
(4) Site of Staircase
   to Upper Floor
(5) Store Rooms
(6) Corridor to South Wing
(7) Store Rooms
(8) Magazines—Store Room
(9) Lightwell
(10) Room with store jars
(11) Caretaker's House
(12) Main Entrance

(B) = HOUSE II

(C) = HOUSE III

(13) Staircase to Upper Floor
(14) Store Rooms
(15) Rooms with Original
   Paving
(16) Corridor to South Wing
(17) Porter's Lodge
(18) Original Threshold

(19) Room with Greek statue base
(20) Large room or shrine
(21) Corridor to North Wing
(22) Filter Basin/Cistern
(23) Open air courtyard
(24) North East Cistern
(25) Greek Altar

LEVIN (LENDAS)

An isolated site, situated along the southern coast, south of Festos and very close to the fishing village of **Lendas.**

LEVIN or **LEBEN** was once a Phoenician outpost from where the name originated (*Leben is a semetic word meaning Lion*) — and came from the promontory that resembles a lion. This promontory is important as it protects the harbour.

Levin was very important during the 6th and 5th centuries BC and was the main harbour of **Gortyna.** It also flourished under the Romans, due to its therapeutic springs with their curative powers and it became a centre of medicine. A sanctuary dedicated to Asklepios,

the God associated with medicine and curative powers, was built here as long ago as the 4th century BC and it was restored in the 2nd century AD.

There are various remains of guest houses, baths for the sick, a well, a portico, some of the Hellenistic era, including a fine mosaic floor, but most of the Roman period.

To the east, are the remains of an 11th century church of **Ayios Ioannis,** erected on the ruins of an earlier Basilica. Some 4kms from the village are the remains of **Circular Minoan Tombs** (*Tholi*) where cycladic figurines and pottery were discovered including jewellery and some show that there were very strong trade connections with Egypt.

MALIA PALACE

The ancient town of Malia is to the east of modern Malia, a major tourist centre, and along the northern coast. **THE PALACE OF MALIA** dates from the Middle Minoan period ≈1900BC. It was destroyed around 1700BC, rebuilt and survived until 1450BC. The existing remains of the Palace and the surrounding houses date to the middle and late Minoan periods. It resembles the other main palaces but has its own individual features.

DESCRIPTION OF THE PALACE

2) Circular Structures — Total of 8 in two groups of 4, each 17 feet across; believed to have been used as granaries.

3) The South Entrance — This was the main entrance and leads to the central court.

4) The Central Court — 52 yards long and 24 yards wide, has different elevations on each side. In the centre is a shallow pit *(bothros)* —(5).

7) Kernos — Circular stone table which some believe was used more for secular than religious purposes. It has 34 small depressions round a large central one.

8) Ceremonial Staircase — a monumental structure.

9) Pillar Crypt — Similar to that of Knossos where cult figures are carved on the pillars —Around it are a number of interconnected rooms.

(12) Leopards Hall — Here are some large pithoi in the various rooms, from one of which an axe-head in the shape of a Leopard was discovered, together with a sword *(Heraklion Museum - Gallery IV)*.

(13) Western Corridor — The room around it believed to be storage rooms.

(14) Palace Archives — Here a hieroglyphic-script and a Linear A tablet were found.

(16) Megaron — Further to the north west —Principal apartments of the Palace including gardens.

(18) The West Court — This has been cleared only recently.

(20) Pillar Hall — This was a large court surrounded with columns which were supporting upper rooms.

(23) Northern Court — Its orientation has been shown to correspond with certain exceptional appearances of the full moon above mount Selena.

(25) North Entrance and a fine paved road —along the way are some large pithoi.

(29) Eastern Complex — to the east of the central court. The magazines were situated behind a portico of alternatively circular and rectangular columns. They were storage places for oil and wine. The magazines are protected in a locked shed.

Malia — The Grand Staircase.

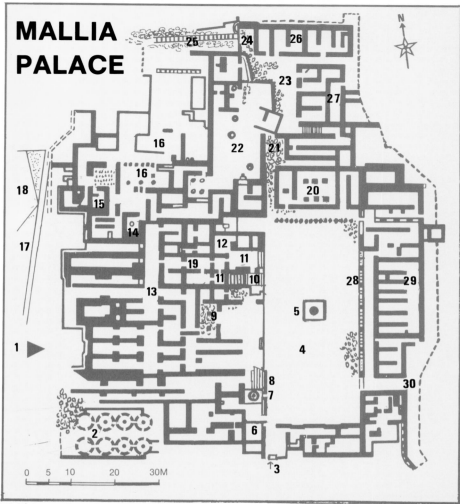

MALLIA PALACE

N

Malia —
the Kernos Circular Stone.

(1) Entrance from Car Park
(2) Storage Silos
(3) South Entrance
(4) CENTRAL COURT
(5) Sacrificial Pit
(6) Antechamber
(7) Kernos-Circular Stone
(8) Ceremonial Staircase
(9) Pillar Crypt
(10) Grand Staircase
(11) Cult Rooms
(12) Leopard's Hall
(13) West Corridor
(14) Palace Archives
(15) Lustral Basin
(16) MEGARON
(17) Procession Road
(18) West Court
(19) Official Rooms
(20) Pillared Hall
(21) Corridor
(22) Tower Courtyard
(23) North Court
(24) North Entrance Hall
(25) Paved Road
(26) Storage Magazines
(27) Storage Magazines
(28) Collonade
(29) Eastern Magazines
(30) East Entrance

THE ANCIENT CITY OF MALIA

The city was occupied during the same period as the palace, and at other times by later civilizations, however these were of a very small scale. Serious excavation started within the area which stretched up to the sea, in the 1960's. The most extensive excavations were carried out in the AGORA area (2) — an open space area of about 40x40 metres, to the north west side of the palace, and to the north west, where is the so called **HYPOSTYLE CRYPT** (2A) — a complex of various rooms, storage magazines and benches. It is protected with a cover.

3) Western Quarters – This is an area with many houses, in the centre of one house there is a lustral basin or bath.

3A) Northwestern Quarter – a large building of the first Palace period. A deposit of hieroglyphic archive came to light in 1968.

11) Early Christian Basilica – ruins about ½ a mile from the palace. Built over a tomb which contained a sarcophagus of the 2nd century AD. The Basilica was built in the 6-7th century AD.

9) House A – of the first Palace period.

12) Khrysolakkos (Pit of Gold) is close to the sea, a large rectangular burial enclosure containing several compartments, believed to be of Royal burials. Some of the finds include a famous gold pendant of two conjoined bees (now at Heraklion Museum). Also it is believed that the famous Aegean treasure now in the British Museum, was actually found here in the 19th century.

Ossuaries, to the north of Khrysolakkos, the rocky coast contains natural caves and in the bay of the small islet of **Ayia Varvara**

remains of the period of the first palace include workshops.

(7) Eastern Quarter – 3 houses have been discovered.

(6) House E – Middle to Late Minoan period, a large house with post Palatial reoccupation.

(5) Sanctuary – This building is believed to have been a shrine.

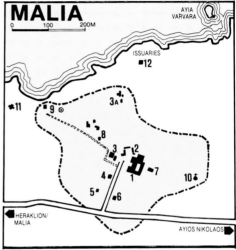

(1) PALACE	(7) Eastern Quarter
(2) Agora	(8) Middle Quarter
(3) Western Quarters	(9) House A
(3A) Northwestern Quarters	(10) Ayios Nikolaos
(4) House B	(11) Early Christian
(5) Sanctuary	Basilica
(6) House E	(12) Khrysolakkos

General view of the ruins of Malia Palace.

MONASTERIES OF THE DISTRICT

MONI AGARATHOS – *Some 22kms south east of Heraklion – west of Kastelli.* Built on the remains of a very old monastic establishment, it is one of the oldest in Crete. During the Venetian period it was an ecclesiastical and intellectual centre and many Scholars and Patriarchs started their careers from here. The first Bishop of a Metropolis – Metropolitan of Crete, **Neophytos Patelaros** had his base here. Many of its treasures and documents were taken to the island of Kithyra. Built high up, it provides panoramic views of the coastline and is surrounded by pine and fir trees and olive groves. A religious fair takes place on 23 April, *St. George's Day.*

MONI APANOSIFI – Some 31kms south of Heraklion. Also called **Ayios Yeoryios Apanosifi** is one of the most important and richest monasteries of the island. It was founded by the monk **Paisios** around 1600. During the Turkish occupation, due to its isolated position it was a revolutionary and intellectual centre. Built on a hill with excellent surroundings, it is an ideal place for an excursion, although getting there from the main tourist centres is not that easy. Limited overnight accommodation is available. There is an excellent collection of religious relics — On 23 April the fair of St. George takes place.

MONI APEZANES – *63kms south of Heraklion,* near the south coast and north of the ancient port of Levin. It is believed that the monastery was originally situated further to the south, in the **Holy Gorge** *(Ayiofrango)* where there is a Byzantine church of **Ayios Antonios,** and moved to its present position for protection from the Crusaders. Some written evidence indicates that the monastery was built around 1458. It was fortified with ramparts and had a cannon. It contains several religious treasures including vestments, crosses, gospels and the remains of 19 Saints.

MONI VRONDISI – *48kms southwest of Heraklion, by the southern slopes of mount Idi.* Due to its high position, some 550 metres, it commands excellent views of the Messara Plain below.

Vrondisi, is a historic and fortified monastery and played a big role in the revolution against the Turks in the 19th century.

At the entrance of the monastery there is a marble fountain of the 15th century of excellent artistic value. It is an Italian style fountain with statues of Adam and Eve and faces of 4 men. Water is running from their mouths.

In the church of **Ayios Antonios** an Apostle **Thomas,** within the monastery there is an old Italian belfry which contai many wall paintings and frescoes. Howevel only a few frescoes survive dating from th 14th century. **Michael Damaskenos,** on of the best of the 16th century Cretan Schoc of painters, was a monk in the monastery.

MONI VARSAMONERO – An ol monastery, only half an hours walk west c Vrondisi Monastery. It is now abandone and only the chapel of **Ayios Fanourio** remains which is very important due to it excellent frescoes, which are amongst th best in Crete and date to the 14th and 15t centuries.

Ayios Fanourios shows Italian influence an is of an unusual form. Here at the monastery there was a thriving artistic school in th 14th, 15th and 16th centuries and man works and icons were produced by the artist including **Constantine Riccos.** Most of th icons and woodcarvings are now on displa at the Historical Museum of Heraklion an others have been removed to Vrondis monastery.

The modern but beautiful church of the monastery of Kalliviani.

98

MONI KERA KARDIOTISSA - to the eastern side of the road, heading towards Lasithi Plain — *some 49kms from Heraklion.* This is an old monastery, the exact date of its origin is not known, but its name comes from a very old icon of Virgin Mary, known as **Kera.** The church is well preserved and a religious fair takes place on 8 September.

The church contains Byzantine style frescoes; the important icon of the Virgin Mary was taken to Italy in 1498 and is still kept in the church of St. Alphonse in Rome.

MONI PALIANI - *20kms south of Heraklion* — The Convent is situated south of the **Venerato** village and houses a large number of nuns who produce excellent hand woven articles which are exhibited permanently and are for sale.

It is one of the oldest cloisters of Crete. The church is dedicated to the Assumption of Virgin Mary. The convent was burnt by the Turks during the revolutions of 1821 and 1866.

MONI ODHIGITRIA - *62kms southwest of Heraklion* and close to the coast, north of the fishing village of **Kali Limenes.** An important historical monastery with fortifications and was once surrounded by a wall for protection. It is situated in an isolated position and was another revolutionary centre against the Turks.

In the nearby legendary castle **"Xopateras"**, Abbot Xopateras was killed fighting with a handful of others against the numerically superior Turkish forces. In the church there are some excellent icons and frescoes.

MONI KALLIVIANIS - This is a modern Convent with some building complexes and extensive gardens. The church has some wall paintings. It is also an orphanage and has excellent workshops and some of the handicrafts are on sale at the permanent collection which is near the main entrance.

Panoramic view of the monastery of Kera Kardiotissa.

THE HERAKLION COUNTRYSIDE

Heraklion is the largest district of Crete, offering enormous contrasts and exciting scenery. Scattered all over the countryside among the vineyards and the olive groves are ruins of the past, some of them well known all over the world.

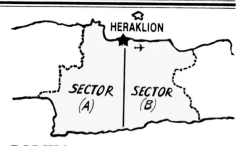

SECTOR (A) — WESTERN SIDE
West of Heraklion

BAY OF RHODIAS – The coast along the bay provides excellent beaches and has a number of hotels and many fish tavernas. The main highway to Rethymno runs parallel to the bay.

AYIA PELAYIA

An expanding tourist area. A picturesque bay between the capes of *Dia* and *Tripiti*. As a tourist resort it has an excellent beach within the bay and commanding views from the hilltops where there are numerous hotels and other types of accommodation. There is also the well known *Capsis Beach Complex;* numerous tavernas and sea sports are available.

Some Minoan and Hellenistic finds have been recovered in the area called **Panormos.**

RODHIA – An inland town near the coast and the beaches. There is a Venetian **Palazzo** *(only the facade survives)* near the church of the village. 5kms to the north of the village in the **Convent of Savathiana** where nuns produce fine handicraft work. The church of **Ayios Antonios** has interesting icons.

ALMYROS OF MALEVIZI – A bottomless lake of unknown depth. The German forces dumped all their vehicles and other armoury before abandoning Crete, but they must have gone so deep, no one has located them yet. There were many windmills on the side, now deserted and destroyed.

The Beautiful Bay of Ayia Pelayia by the Kapsis Beach Complex.

FODHELE – A village to the north side, believed to have been the birthplace of the most famous of Cretans **EL-GRECO**. It has a very mild climate and is rich in citrus, fruit and vegetable products.

Tel: Community: (081) 280 688.

EL-GRECO *(THE GREEK)*

By name **Dominicos Theotokopoulos** was born in 1541 and died on 7/4/1614. He studied religious painting at the school of "Mount Sinai" at Heraklion and went to Venice and thereafter to Rome in 1570. There he became a student of Titian but moved to Spain in 1577 where he settled in **Toledo** and stayed for the remainder of his life. It was there that he produced his masterpieces.

In 1934 the Spanish University of Valiadilis erected a plaque here hewn from the rock of Toledo written in Greek and Spanish and reads:

> *The School of History of the University of Valiadilis Palm in the heart of Castalia, presents to Fodele this plaque hewn from the Rock of Toledo. In memory of the glory of Dominicos Theotoko-poulos July 1934.*

El Greco's statue at Fodhele.

SOUTH OF HERAKLION

AYIOS MIRON – A centre of the region with a Venetian style 13th century church. Nearby is ancient **RAVKOS** or **RAFXOS**. It was an independent state with its own mint.

A church at the centre of Ayia Varvara Village.

RIZINIA – An ancient site, known as **PRINIAS**. Now there is the small village of Prinias from where it is the best way to approach the ancient site.

The Acropolis called **Patela** is situated on the top of a large rocky table. There were fortifications and two Archaic Temples of the 7 to 6th centuries BC. The original inhabitants were Minoans then it was settled by the Dorian Greeks. Various finds including figures of seated goddesses and horses with riders are now at Heraklion Museum.

AYIA VARVARA – A large village, an agricultural centre of the area and with a fine church by the square. To the west of the village there is a huge rock with a chapel at the top, dedicated to **Prophitis Elias.** The rock is called **Omphallos** – *(in phalic symbol shape)*. It is believed that this is the spiritual centre and a balancing point of the island.

MESSARA – The largest flat area of Crete, about 30kms in length and 5kms in width. A very fertile land and since ancient times it has supplied Crete with cereals, vegetables and other agricultural products. Modern farming and methods of irrigation have ensured much wealth to the area.

MIRES – This is the agricultural centre of the area, a rich town with many shops, bus connections and some basic accommodation.

Tel: Munincipality: (0892) 22251.

101

HERAKLION DISTRICT
(NOMOS HERAKLIOU) –
2,641 square kms.

The District *(Nomos)* of Heraklion is in fact the central part of the island; the centre of all communications and the tourist's premier choice. Apart from the fame of the excellent beaches of Ayia Pelagia, Hersonissos, Malia and Matala, people come here to explore the famous Heraklion Museum and the world famous centre of the Minoan civilisation, that of Knossos.

Akr. Stavros

To SANDORINI

AYIA PELAYIA
Tripiti
Ornos Rodhias

Sisses
Achla'da
Fodhele
Moni Savathianou
Moni Ayiou Pandeleimon
Rodhia

Stroumboulas
Ammoudara

Tilisos
TYLISSOS Kalesia

OROS IDI
(Psiloritis)

Gonies
Sklavokambos
Korfes
Voutes
Anoyia

Profit
Rafkos

Timios Stavros (2,456m.)
Krousonas
Dafnes
Skinakas
Ayios Miron

IDEON ANDRON
Moni Ayia Ireni
Temenos
Castro
Asites
Venerato
Moni PALIANI

Ampelakia
RIZINIA
Prinias

Platanos
Moni VARSAMONERO
Ayios Thomas

Kamares
Moni VRONDISI
Ayia Varvara
Dam

Grigoria
ZAROS
Gergeri

Makarikaki
Klima
Larani

Moni KERA KARDIOTISSA
Galia

Ayia Galini
Timbaki
Vori
GORTYS

Kokkinos Pyrgos
Moni KALLIVIANIS
Ambelouzos
Galates
Soka

KOLPOS
MESSARA
AYIA
TRIADA
FESTOS
Mires
Ayii Dheka
Stoll

Kommo
Ayios Ioannis
Platanos
Vagionia
Sterr

Pombia
Vivi
(Tombs of Mesara)

Pitsidia
Sivas

MATALA
Matala

Moni APEZANES
Kofinas
Moni Koudo

Moni ODHIGITRIA
Antiskari

KALI LIMENES
LEVIN
Lendas

Lasea
Akr. Lithino
N. Megalonissi
N. Papadoplaka

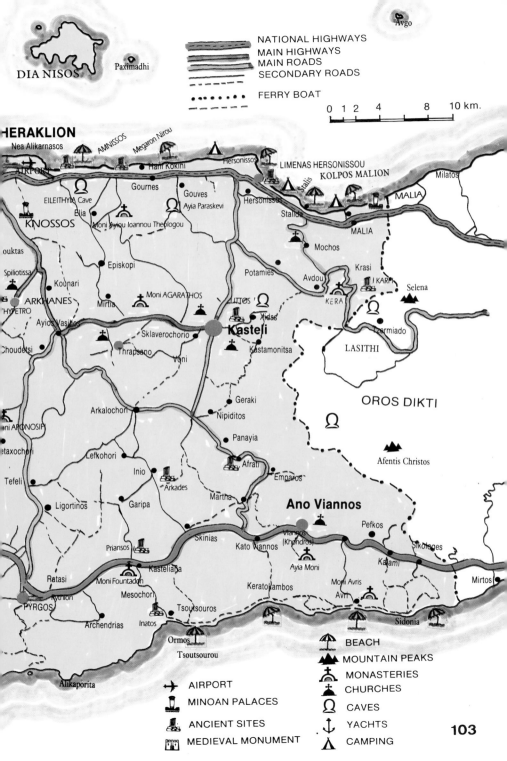

DIA NISOS
Paximadhi
Avgo

NATIONAL HIGHWAYS
MAIN HIGHWAYS
MAIN ROADS
SECONDARY ROADS
FERRY BOAT

0 1 2 4 8 10 km.

HERAKLION
Nea Alikarnasos
AMNISSOS
Megaron Nirou
Hani Kokini
Hersonissos
LIMENAS HERSONISSOU
KOLPOS MALION
Milatos
AIRPORT
Stalis
Gournes
Gouves
Hersonissos
MALIA
EILEITHYIA Cave
Ayia Paraskevi
Stalida
Elia
KNOSSOS
Moni Ayiou Ioannou Theologou
MALIA
Mochos
ouktas
Episkopi
Krasi
Spiliotissa
Potamies
Avdou
KARFI
Kounari
Selena
ARKHANES
Mirtia
Moni AGARATHOS
KERA
HYPETRO
LIOS
Tzermiado
Ayios Vasilios
Sklaverochorio
Xidas
Kasteli
LASITHI
Choudetsi
Thrapsano
Kastamonitsa
Voni
OROS DIKTI
Geraki
Arkalochori
Nipiditos
ni APONOSIFI
Panayia
Afentis Christos
etaxochori
Lefkohori
Inio
Afrati
Tefeli
Arkades
Emparos
Ligortinos
Garipa
Martha
Ano Viannos
Skinias
Pefkos
Priansos
Kato Viannos
Viannos
(Khondros)
Sikologos
Ratasi
Kasteliana
Ayia Moni
Kalami
Moni Fountadon
Keratokambos
Moni Avris
Mirtos
Kythion
Mesochori
Avri
PYRGOS
Tsoutsouros
Sidonia
Archendrias
Inatos
Ormos
Tsoutsourou
BEACH
Alikaporita
MOUNTAIN PEAKS
MONASTERIES
AIRPORT
CHURCHES
MINOAN PALACES
CAVES
ANCIENT SITES
YACHTS
MEDIEVAL MONUMENT
CAMPING

103

AYII DHEKA *("Holy Ten")* – A village, just to the east of the ancient site of **Gortyna**. The name derives from "Ten Martyrs" — 10 Christians who were killed by the Romans in the 3rd century AD for their beliefs. Many of the houses in the village incorporate old columns and stones taken from the ancient city.

AYIOS IOANNIS – A village close to the ancient site of Festos. It has an old chapel of **Ayios Pavlos** with one of the most unique 14th century architectural forms in Crete. There are old frescoes and icons within.

KOMMO BEACH is close to the village of **Pitsidia**. *KOMMO* was the ancient port town of Festos. Recent finds have revealed an increasingly interesting archaeological site, which can only be reached by a truck road. There is a group of fine Minoan Houses, a Temple and a sanctuary from the Classical-Hellenistic periods.

MATALA   Tel: OTE (0892) 2220

An expanding tourist town, first discovered b the hippies as a lonely paradise. Caves *(see below* were used as their living quarters during thei long stay. When other tourists started arrivin the hippies moved out and Matala became respectable resort open to all, with hotel tavernas and a camping site and an exceller market. It attracts people of all ages but youn, people predominate. Its fine beach provide excellent bathing.

THE CAVES are on the northern side of th Cove, a massive cliff where hundreds o caves were carved out by man, althoug nobody knows whether it was the Minoans the Classical Greeks or the Romans.

Matala was used as a port of Gortyna and b the edge of the cliffs there are underwate remains. The coast to the south is very interesting and local fishermen can take yo to explore the various grottoes (for reasonable fee).

Matala attracts many people

THE SOUTH COAST

has many coves and bays, some sandy, but it is almost inaccessible except to the following:

KALI LIMENES – (Fair Harbour) — Not very well connected but worth a visit. This isolated fishing village is picturesque and has good beaches. Here it is believed St. Paul came ashore in AD60 on his way to Rome from Caesaria.

LEBEN (LENDAS) – *see also archaeological sites.* Connected with Gortys, was once its main port. An isolated fishing village with a good beach and famous for its springs which have curative powers, ideal for ulcers. The climate is excellent and even attracts swallows all the year round.

THE MESSARA TOMBS

– These are various tombs scattered around the area of Messara, southern side up to the coast. This proves that the whole area was habitated in ancient times and the many finds show connections both trading and cultural with Egypt, Babylonia, Cyprus and the Aegean Islands. Some of the finds include personalised seals of seal stones, some of precious metals.

General view of Leben (Lendas)

BETWEEN MESARA AND MOUNT IDI

ZAROS – Has famous springs and it is a stopping place for those wishing to explore the mountains – *see under Rethymnon.* About 2kms from Zaros is the monastic settlement of **Ayios Nikolaos,** a cave on the side of the ravine with 15th century frescoes and icons and an altar from the Renaissance period. The monasteries of **Valsamonerou** and **Ayiou Vrondisiou,** both close by are described in the monasteries section.

KAMARES – This is a centre for climbers and explorers. There is accommodation and eating facilities, mules and guides can be hired for the explorers.

Even to explore the nearest cave of **Kamares** which is to the north of the town, it takes about 4 hours walk one way, which means that an overnight stay is essential. The cave was discovered by a local shepherd in the 1890's and has shown that it was used in the Neolithic period and that it was a sacred place for the Minoans. Various offerings, presumably to the Gods were discovered and are on display at Heraklion Museum.

IDEO ANDRO – One of Crete's most famous Caves can be reached from Kamares or perhaps easier from **Anoyia** — *see under Rethymnon* from where we understand a new road is being built. The cave has an entrance, 9 metres high and 27 metres wide. Inside there are several chambers, the biggest being 36x34 metres. Many of the items discovered inside the cave include bronze shields, spears, cups, tripods, from the 9 to 8th centuries BC some showing Assyrian influence, unique in Crete.

The Cave was the centre of the **Cult of the GURETES** *(Warriors)* of the Dorian Greeks.

MOUNT IOUKTAS – A mountain peak with a profile of **ZEUS** — *"The Sleeping Zeus"* as can be seen from Heraklion and the coast. It makes an interesting trip to the peak and views from there are splendid.

It is situated to the north of Arkhanes, an ancient place *(see archaeological sites)*. There are ancient caves dating to the neolithic and Neo-Palatial periods and at the peak there is a Minoan sanctuary with remains of a massive temenos wall. At the peak there is also a chapel of **Afendis Christos** *(Lord Christ)* and celebrations take place on 6 August. For those wishing to explore the area, guides are available at Arkhanes.

Below: Mount Iouktas as seen from Heraklion — The Sleeping Zeus.

ARKHANES *(see also archaeological sites).* The modern town is large and prosperous, rich in agricultural products including grapes. There are in fact two Arkhanes, *Kato Arkhanes,* to the north and the main town further south, *Epano Arkhanes* which we refer to as Arkhanes. The church of **Panayia** contains an excellent collection of icons and **Ayia Triada** church contains some Byzantine frescoes.

Close to Arkhanes is the church of **Michael Asomatos** and contains excellent 14th century frescoes of the Cretan school including a striking crusifixion and the capture of Jericho.

Tel: Police: (081) 751 811
   Munincipality: 751 898

VATHYPETRO – South of Arkhanes, this is breathtaking countryside and can be reached by a rough road. Recent excavations revealed ancient habitation dating back to the Chalkolithic period. Other finds from the first half of the 6th century BC have shown a building with a central court, main hall, terraces, sacred chambers and a basement where pottery workshops, weaving rooms, oil & wine presses and store rooms with large pithoi were found. Perhaps a Minoan villa. The place is locked.

SECTOR (B) — EASTERN SIDE
EAST OF HERAKLION

KATSAMBA – Some 2kms east of Heraklion, on the way to the airport and by the mouth of the now dry Kairatos river, was the ancient harbour of Knossos. Remains of tombs from the Neolithic to the Minoan periods were found. A vase found here has descriptions of a cartouche of Pharoah Tuthmosis III. Another find is an ivory pyxis, both on display at Heraklion Museum *Cases 82 & 71A*.

AMNISOS – A Minoan Palace settlement, believed to be a port or a naval headquarters of Knossos. From here, Idomeneas sailed with his ships to the Trojan Wars. Finds include an Archaic Circular Altar *(sanctuary)* of **Zeus Thenatas,** a villa of the Lillies, with good frescoes depicting Lillies, believed to have been the home of the port commander. The place was mentioned in Linear B tablets.

It was a prosperous 16th century Venetian village and now has been developed into a sizeable tourist area with a good beach, hotels and apartments.

CAVE OF EILEITHYIA *("The Womb of the Earth")* also known to locals as **Neraid-hospilios.** It was used as a burial site, also a shrine in Neolithic and Minoan times, as a sacred spot dedicated to Nature Goddess and to **Eileithyia** *"Liberator"*, goddess of childbirth in particular and protector of women in general.

According to ODYSSEY XIX, "Odysseas, disguised as a beggar lied to Penelope and claimed that Odysseas was put in Amnisos . . where the cave of Eileithyia is situated . . ." The cave has fine stalactites but is locked for protection. However the key can be obtained from the caretaker at the village.

NIROU – A tourist village by the coast, with a fine beach and hotels. Here are the remains of a **Minoan Megaron** but of no great interest although some of the finds including double axes, seals, jewellery, bronze vessels, oil lamps, vases etc, *(now at Heraklion Museum)* are of some interest. There are submerged columns and bases of the old harbour to be seen and there are rock cut tombs in the area.

HERSONISSOS

Also known as **Limin Hersonissou** is probably the biggest modern tourist town in Crete, attracting many visitors, with accommodation varying, from the simplest single room type to the luxurious deluxe hotel complex.

The small harbour is picturesque and the beaches and coves are sandy and shallow. Various watersports, sailing, skiing and wind-surfing are available. Tavernas and cafes provide eating and relaxing places and shops display excellent souvenirs, crafts, and jewellery. There are numerous discotheques.

ANCIENT HERSONISSOS was a thriving seaport, mainly during the Hellenistic period (founded in the 5th century BC) and its prosperity continued during the Roman and

View of Hersonissos main Beach.

early Byzantine years. Submerged remains can be seen near the harbour and small finds from houses were found in many fields, but much of the old city is buried, perhaps, under the modern town.

There was a famous Temple of *Artemis Britomarts* and during the early Christian era it was a seat of a Bishop and remains of an early Christian Basilica were found by the harbour with some mosaic floors. Limin Hersonissou was the harbour of the inland city of LYTTOS.

The village, prior to the tourist expansion is about 1 mile inland on the hilltop overlooking the bay, thus providing panoramic views. More tourist complexes are in and around the villag and the area between here and the sea scattered with ancient ruins mainly belo ground.

Tel: Community: (0897) 22 202
   Police: 22 222

MALIA – Another popular tourist town wit an excellent beach and plentiful hot accommodation, tavernas and night life. Th ancient Palace of Malia is to the east side o the modern town and is fully describe under archaeological sites.

Tel: Community (0897) 31 265

Above: The small harbour of Hersonissos. *Below:* General view of the sandy Malia Beach.

POTAMIES - Along the road to Lasithi. The little Byzantine church of **Christos** contains restored frescoes. The old monastery of **Panayia Gouverniotissa**, 10th century, is now deserted but its church contains 14th century frescoes.

KRASSI *(KRASSION)* - An ideal place to stop for a rest as it is buried in greenery. There is here a remarkable, gigantic plane tree nourished by the endless running springs. Nearby is the monastery of **Panayia Kera** *(see monasteries)*

KARPHI *(Nail)* - A sharp rising peak, some 1100 metres in height. At the top of the peak there is a very important Minoan settlement which was established after the final destruction of the Palaces c1450BC. Perhaps it was chosen by Minoans as a refuge, because of its isolated position. Although a refuge from people, it was open to the elements of nature such as winds and snow, thus was later abandoned. There was a temple, a tower etc *(refer to map)*.

Near Potamies.

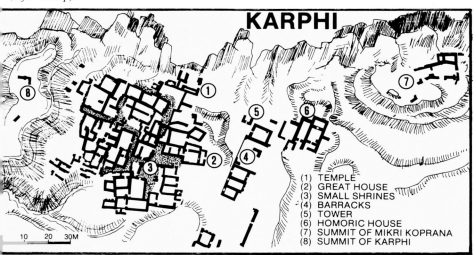

KARPHI

10 20 30M

(1) TEMPLE
(2) GREAT HOUSE
(3) SMALL SHRINES
(4) BARRACKS
(5) TOWER
(6) HOMORIC HOUSE
(7) SUMMIT OF MIKRI KOPRANA
(8) SUMMIT OF KARPHI

AYIOS VASILIOS - The village with a church of **John the Baptist** containing 13th century frescoes. Nearby is the small monastery of **Epanosiffi** where the church of **Ayios Yeoryios** dates to 1600 and has an excellent octagonal fountain.

THRASPANO - A village which has kept the old traditions of hand made earthenware pottery and ceramics.

KLAVEROCHORIO - The church of the **Presentation of the Virgin** has good frescoes of the Cretan School dating to the 15-16th centuries.

KASTELLI - The centre of the south eastern region. The Byzantine church of **Eisodhia Theotokon** dating to 10th century incorporates some ancient columns. It is a well preserved church and contains frescoes and icons including a dramatic scene of the *Transfiguration of St. Francis*. To the north is **Ayios Panteleimon** church, an unusual structure in a wonderful setting of oak trees.

Here there was a 13th century Venetian-Genoese castle which has now been destroyed. It was used once as a headquarters by Omar Pasha, 1867.

Tel: Police (0891) 31233 Community 31266

109

LYTTOS (or TYKTOS) — An ancient city to the east of Kastell. It was a Hellenistic town of great importance and had its own mint and was using Hersonissos to the north as its own harbour. It was destroyed in c220BC and little is to be found except the remains of an early large Byzantine Basilica.

ARKALOCHORI – A market village in the centre of the eastern region. Here, an ancient settlement existed and there are caves of the late-Minoan period and other tombs. Many valuable finds were discovered including bronze weapons, double axes in gold-bronze and silver, vases and swords some with linear A inscriptions.

AFRATI – A small village to the west of which is the site of ancient **ARKADES** situated on a hilltop; a Dorian settlement where many tombs and a sanctuary of the 9-8th century BC were discovered.

ANO VIANNOS – A large picturesque village, nicely situated to the south eastern corner of the region with vast olive groves and vineyards.

The church of **Ayia Pelayia** and **Ayio Yeoryios** contain frescoes and icons of th 14 and 15th centuries. 2-3 miles out is th ancient site of **KHONDROS** (ancien VIANNOS), an important late Minoan II site with extensive remains of houses wa found.

AVRI (or ARVI) – A small isolated fishin village of almost tropical climate, ideal fo the growing of bananas. The **gorge of Avr** has an ancient legend from mythology *"Zeus struck the rocky cliff to open a passag for the water to flow . . . ''* When there is high wind, the noise of the water rushing sounds like a titanic thunder. The presen church of the village is built on th foundations of an ancient Temple of Zeus.

The place attracts young people due to it isolated position. There's some hotel an apartment accommodation and good beache

Nearby is the now abandoned but onc flourishing monastery of **Ayios Antonios**

KERATOKAMBOS – An isolated, excel lent and well protected beach, south of An Viannos. On the top of a sharp rising roc *(some 600 metres above sea level)* are the ruin of a post-Minoan village.

The **gorge of Avri**

HERAKLION — USEFUL INFORMATION

SERVICES WITHIN THE DISTRICT OF HERAKLION

STATION 1 — Georgiadou 6 Street — OASIS — Tel. 288 544
   To: East and South East regions: KASTELLI-PYRGOS & VIANNOS.
STATION 2 — Platia Koraka *(Hanioporta)* Tel. 283 073
   To: West, South & South West regions: ARKHANES-AYIOS MIRON—MIRES—
        VORI etc/FESTOS—MATALA—KAMARES.
STATION 3 — Machi tis Kritis Street (Hanioporta) Tel. 283 287
   To: West region: TYLISSOS — ANOYIA.
STATION 4 — Megaro Fytaki — HARBOUR Tel. 282 637.
   To: East region: HERSONISSOS—MALIA—LASITHI PLAIN

BUS SERVICES CONNECTING THE REST OF CRETE

EAST CRETE: Tel. 283 338 from HARBOUR STATION
   To: HERSONISSOS — MALIA — NEAPOLIS — AYIOS NIKOLAOS
              GOURNIA — IERAPETRA — SITIA
WEST CRETE: Tel. 283 338 from HARBOUR station & MAKARIOU ST.
              Tel. 221 765.
   To: PERAMA—RETHYMNO — GEORGOUPOLI — HANIA.
SOUTH CRETE: Tel. 283 338 from HARBOUR station & MAHI KRITIS St. (HANIO-
              PORTA) Tel. 283 073.
   To: GORTYS — MIRES — FESTOS — AYIA TRIADA — MATALA —AYIA
              GALINNI
Distances: To Ayios Nikolaos 65kms — Sitia 113kms — Rethymno 79kms — Hania 137kms.

BEACHES OF HERAKLION DISTRICT

Heraklion is not only the most important place for ancient sites but it also provides some of the most extensive and popular beaches, most of them providing excellent waters and many water sports and activities.

Along the northern coast from west to the east are: **AYIA PELAYIA, LINOPERAMATA, AMMOUDARA** all west of Heraklion and easy to reach by bus, coach or car.

AMNISOS, PACHIA AMMOS, NIROU, HERSONISSOS, STALLS MALIA are all to the east of Heraklion and can easily be reached by bus.

EOT *(Greek Tourist Organisation beach)* is a public beach east of Heraklion with all facilities and a small entrance fee. Along the southern coast, the most important and popular is the beach of **MATALA**, west side and to a lesser degree **KOKKINOS PIRGOS, KALI LIMENES, LEVIN** and **AVRI** on the eastern side. However, most of the southern coast with the small coves and bays is isolated and mountainous.

ACCOMMODATION

All the above mentioned popular beaches on the northern side and Matala on the south, have accommodation to satisfy all pockets and all requirements, ranging from cheap room accommodation or apartments, self catering complexes some with swimming pools and hotels of all categories right up to the most luxurious tourist complexes.

A complete guide featuring all the hotels can be obtained from the Greek National Tourist Organisation or from the **Association of Hoteliers of Crete:** Idomeneos & Malikouti Street, Heraklion-Crete, Tel. (081) 223967 Telex 262380. *They also provide a list of Cretan Tour Operators.*

111

CAMPING

There are well organised camping sites at Hersonissos, Couves, Ammoudara, Matala and Malia. For any further information about camping accommodation and facilities in either Crete or Greece, please apply to the **GREEK CAMPING ASSOCIATION** — 102 Solonos Street, Athens. Tel. 3621560/3613941.

AMMOUDARA: Heraklion Camping. Tel. 283 164 — Up to 850 people; by the beach ... all amenities.

GOUVES: Crete Camping: (0897) 41400. Up to 270 people; by the beach.

HERSONISSOS: Caravan Camping 771 285. Up to 100 people; by the beach.

MALIA: Malia Camping (0897) 31460. Up to 500 people; by the beach.

MATALA: Matala Camping (0892) 42340 around 300 people; by the beach.

The **YOUTH HOSTEL** is at 24 Handakos Street—Heraklion

FESTIVALS

Wine Festival in July at Dafnes Demenous lasting for 10 days. Free wine, Cretan dancing and singing and delicious food. Exhibitions also take place. Inf. Tel: (081) 791 256.

Wine Festival at Sarchos Malevias. End of May around the well known cave of Sarchos. Info: (081) 711575.

Immigrants Festival: 6-8 August at Kastelli Pediadas, with events of dancing, folklore, theatre etc. Tel. (0891) 31 266.

Hersonissia: Annual festival at Hersonissos every August with traditional Cretan eating, drinking, singing, exhibitions etc. Tel. (0897) 22288.

Cretan Panygire — 15 August at Mochos Pediadas. Also on Clean Monday. Info. Tel. (0897) 61325.

Afrati Pediadas Festival: 19-20 July with Cretan folklore.

Cretans in National costumes on parade.

General view of Ayios Nicolaos Harbour.

AYIOS NICOLAOS

This is the administrative centre of the district, a small but very picturesque town, full of character, bustling with life during the tourist season but still very attractive and ideal for a holiday. It is the centre for exploring the fascinating coastline and Mirabello Bay.

Boats in the north side of the lake.

113

HISTORY

A comparatively new town, which started to expand in the last 20 years. However, there are some signs of ancient habitation and it was called **Lato** in the Hellenistic period; no records of the Roman period exist and very few of the Byzantine years.

The Genoese built a castle called **CASTELLO.** It was renamed by the venetians as **MIRA-BELLO** and a small community was established around the garrison. A local uprising headed by *Leon Kallergis* took over the castle for a short period between 1341-1347.

When the Castle of SPINALONGA *(see below)* was built, the Castle of Mirabello was abandoned and eventually destroyed (or crumbled).

Although in 1900 only about 500 inhabitants were registered, by 1905 it became the capital of the district. But it remained a small and sleepy harbour town until the early 1960's when it was discovered by the tourists and ever since it has attracted people from all walks of life, even film producers.

Above: An old photograph showing Ayios Nicolaos *(H. Panteris Collection). Below:* A famous lake and in the far end is the island of Megalonissi which is a natural protection to the harbour.

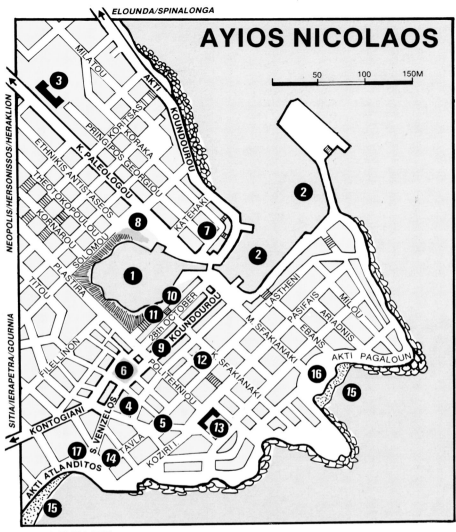

AYIOS NICOLAOS

ELOUNDA/SPINALONGA

NEOPOLIS/HERSONISSOS/HERAKLION

SITIA/IERAPETRA/GOURNIA

50 100 150M

(1) THE LAKE
(2) THE HARBOUR
(3) MUSEUM
(4) Holy Trinity Cathedral
(5) Church of "Our Lady Maria"
(6) Eleftherios Venizelos Square
(7) Youth Hostel
(8) Coach & Car Park
(9) Olympic Airways
(10) Post Office
(11) Tourist Information Office &
     Tourist Police
(12) O.T.E. (Telephones)
(13) Prefecture
(14) BUS STATION to all destinations
(15) Beach
(16) Pagaloun Square
(17) Atlanditos Square

View of Mirabello Bay from Akti Atlanditos

115

PLACES OF INTEREST

There are within the town itself narrow streets, excellent shops, tavernas. Outside there are some beaches, the rocky coastline and the wonderful Mirabello Bay. There is a tremendous atmosphere that is full of life.

THE LAKE – This is not only the most important landmark of Ayios Nicolaos, but it also attracts people from all over Crete. It is called XERATOMENI *(Bottomless)* or VOULLISMENI *(sunken)* Lake and in 1867 it was joined with the sea by a canal.

A strange lake, the source of which is unknown as is its depth. Some believe it to be 210 feet, but nobody knows for sure. One theory is that it is connected with underwater rivers.

According to an old legend, Athena and Artemis Britomartis bathed in the Lake.

The best views of the lake are from the western side, above the cliff. Also by sitting in one of the numerous cafes and tavernas situated around the lake with a drink or a meal.

THE HARBOUR – To the east of the Lake is the picturesque harbour, full of caiques sailing boats and fishing boats. From here you can explore the **Gulf of Mirabello** and the surrounding coast by boat. Other services go to **Elounda Beach** and **Spinalonga Castle** on day trip cruises. There is also a weekly service to Rhodes.

In front of the harbour, acting as natural break waters are the small islets: **MIKRONISSI** *(small islet)* with a lighthouse and **MEGALONISSI** *(large islet)* with the Church of **All Saints.** A religious feast takes place on June 9th and decorated boats ferry pilgrims to the island. This is a very festive occasion.

THE MUSEUM – This is a small museum (with plans for expansion). The main collection consists of Minoan objects found in various places of Eastern Crete. Other exhibits cover other periods up to the Venetian Era.

A small beach-bay by Ayios Nicolaos.

ARCHAEOLOGICAL SITES

OLOUS – This is the port of ancient **Dreros** but very little can be seen except for the remains of a Temple and an early Christian Basilica together with some mosaic floors, also lots of scattered pottery. In ancient times there was continuous conflict with nearby **LATO**. A treaty was established with Rhodes in 200BC. It is situated along the Isthmus over the bridge of Elounda and most of the ruins are submerged.

LATO – A post Minoan site with a Doric settlement dating 7th century BC. Most of the remaining ruins date from the Classic and Hellenistic periods, 5th-3rd cent. BC, when it was a prosperous city.

It's extensive remains include an amphitheatre, fortifications, houses, shops, the Agora, a stoa, cisterns and roads. To the south of the market place with a pronaos is the 2nd cent. BC Temple of Apollo.

The glorious views of Mirabello Gulf and the surrounding area are best enjoyed from the highest spot where the ancient Ákropolis used to be. The site is close to the village of Kritsa with its famous church.

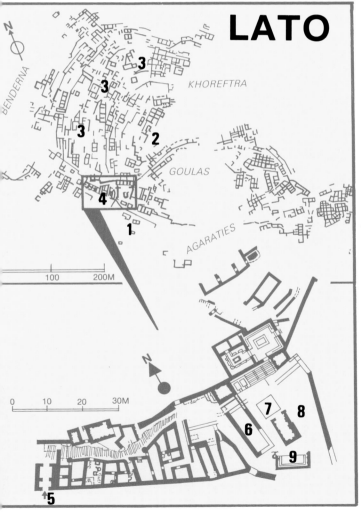

ANCIENT CITY OF
LATO

(1) Temple
(2) Northern Acropolis
(3) Ruins of the City
(4) Enlarged Area
(5) Entrance to enlarged area
(6) Stoa
(7) Agora
(8) Sanctuary
(9) Exedra

117

GOURNIA

The name derives from **GOURNI**, small troughs from which barnyard animals drink — considerable numbers of which were found here.

It was an early Minoan settlement and by 1600BC was a flourishing town with its own ruler and administration. Although it was linked with the other Minoan centres, it functioned as an independent area, a self-contained town which declined at the same time as all the other Minoan centres.

It was around 1900 when work was started by the young American archaeologist Miss Harriet Boyd and by 1904 the whole town was discovered. One of the interesting characteristics is that this ancient Minoan city is so similar in layout to many of Crete's villages.

The site is basically a limestone ridge sprawling over the hillside and no fortifications were discovered.

THE MINOAN PALACE (6) is small in comparison to the other palaces of Crete, possibly used as the general's residence. It was situated on the high point of the Akropolis and had three storeys including a banqueting hall, apartments, courtyards; pillars and stairways.

SANCTUARY (11). This was a small sanctuary where Mother Goddess was worshipped. Many cult objects including terracottas, figures with snakes, doves etc. were found.

THE TOWN with its numerous narrow streets and the small houses *(many reconstructed)* give an extensive graphical idea of what the town looked like in those ancient Minoan years. They include a square, altars for worship and other buildings where they used to live and work.

The rich domestic finds gave an excellent account of the daily life and domestic economy including a forge with moulds for casting chisels, nails, loom weights, a carpenters kit and many other items; all, are now exhibited at Heraklion Museum.

General view of Gournia and the Gulf of Mirabella in the background.

GOURNIA.

(1) ENTRANCE
(2) East Ascent
(3) East Ridge Road
(4) West Ridge Road
(5) Shrine or Sanctuary
(6) Palace
(7) Open Court
(8) Staircase into Palace
(9) Central Hall of Palace
(10) Stores & Magazines
(11) Shrine
(12) Tourist Pavillion

ZAKROS

This is a recent major discovery in a rather isolated part of the eastern coast of Crete which has now been opened up with a good road. Originally it was excavated on a small scale by the British archaeologist D.G. Hoggarth in 1901. Just before the 2nd World War there were some important finds. Immediately after the war, the Greek Department of Antiquities started preliminary excavations but it was in the 1960's that systematic work started, with the assistance of the Greek Government and the American family of *Leon Pomerance*. Then the 4th great Minoan Centre of Crete came to light, much to the excitement of scholars of the Minoan civilisation. Excavations have continued ever since.

The main site is the **PALACE** and the town to the north. To the east is the harbour although this is believed to be submerged under water. Other excavations carried out in the surrounding area, including the *Valley of Death* with its caves and a large Minoan villa close to the village of Ano Zakros, show that the whole area was inhabited.

Habitation in Zakros dates to 2600BC and the Palace dates to 1600BC. This was abandoned in 1450BC. An earlier palace has been found under the foundations of the later Palace.

Zakros was a prosperous outpost of Minoan culture and a major trading centre with the Eastern Mediterranean. There were connections with Egypt, the Levant and Cyprus for the import of Copper.

The PALACE, at its height had 250-300 rooms on either 2 or 3 storeys and was the same architectural type as the other Minoan Palaces. A large cistern (20) and a fountain (21) which were inside the palace and tapped water into the water supply are unique to this palace.

In 1500BC a major disaster occurred *(an earthquake or a tidal wave)*, which destroyed the palace. It was rebuilt, only to be ruined again in 1450BC at the same time as all other Minoan Palaces. (Perhaps, an event related to volcanic eruptions of Santorini which resulted in ash fall-outs and tidal waves). The destruction at Zakros was so sudden that the people left behind very valuable items which were then covered by ash, only to be revealed to us during the recent excavations.

These important items include metal artifacts, cast iron tools, fine swords, large copper ingots, ivory tusks, thousands of vases, large pithoi and some 55 stone vessels. Most of them are now on display at Heraklion Museum.

After 1450BC, the Palace remained abandoned although the town recovered and was inhabited henceforth by people for many years.

Archaeologists however are still mystified as to why the palace was never rebuilt or used again.

General view of the ruins of Zakros Palace *(G.T.O.)*

KATO ZAKROS
PALACE

(1) Main Entrance (Minoan Road to Harbour)
(2) North East Gate
(3) Courtyard
(4) Central Courtyard

A WEST WING
(5) Entrance to West Wing
(6) Anteroom
(7) Lobby
(8) Storerooms
(9) Priest's Rooms
(10) Archive Room
(11) Extension of Works and Dye House
(12) Shrine & Lustral Basin
(13) Treasury
(14) Store Room
(15) Hall of Ceremonies
(16) Banquet Hall

B EAST WING
(17) King's Rooms
(18) Queen's Rooms
(19) Bathroom
(20) Hall of the Cistren
(21) Well of the Fountain
(22) Second Well

C NORTH WING
(23) Kitchen
(24) Store Rooms
(25) Staircase to Dining Room

D SOUTH WING
(26) Sitting Room
(27) Workshops
(28) RESIDENTIAL COMPLEX

121

Part view of the ancient town of Itanos — an idyllic place to visit.

ITANOS - A Minoan settlement to the northern most part of Crete's eastern coast which seemed to have flourished during the Hellenistic, Roman and early Byzantine years. Little remains of its ancient glory and is called by local people as *ERIMOUPOLIS (Deserted City).* Under the Ptolemaic period it served as a naval base. The cemetery is to the north and contains a fine stone-built tomb of the Hellenistic period.

The area is fascinating and provides an exciting excursion as it is not far from the picturesque VAI Bay.

PRESSOS - An ancient city spread across three small hills and was one of the chief post Minoan settlements of Crete. The surviving Minoan farmhouse and tombs show that it was already in existence during the Minoan period but it mainly flourished during the Hellenistic periods.

There are remains of a Hellenistic Akropolis and a large house. Three inscriptions which date between 600-300BC have puzzled many archaeologists. They have Greek characters but with a non-Greek language; some believe them to be the Eteocretan language, others of the Semitic family. Other finds are spread around the nearby villages of Tourtoula, Sklavi and Fourtoulas. The city, according to Strabo, was destroyed in 155BC.

MONASTERIES

MONI PANAYIA KRISTALLENIA –

33kms west of Ayios Nikolaos. It is situated on the eastern part of Lasithi Plain, built on a rocky hill some 840 metres in height and surrounded by fruit trees, almonds, apples and chestnuts. It was destroyed by the Turks due to its revolutionary activities. A religious fare takes place on 15 August.

MONI PANAYIA FANEROMENI –

23kms south east of Ayios Nikolaos. It was founded around the 14th century and commands a fascinating view of the coastline and the Mirabello Bay. In 1538 it was destroyed by the Pirate *Barbarossa* and in 1829 was besieged by the Turks. Now it is a small monastery with a serving church and belongs to Toplou monastery.

MONI KAPSAS – along the eastern side of

the south coast, 41kms from Ayios Nikolaos. It was founded around the 15th century and is built on a steep gorge overlooking the Libyan sea and provides magnificent views.

Originally the monastery was a small church with some cells, expanded later and restored by Ioannis Vitzentas in the 19th century when interesting wall-paintings were added. The wood-engraved temple of the church is one of the best in Crete.

The Famous Monastery of Toplou.

MONI TOPLOU – *20kms east of Sitia.*

It is also known as **Panayia Akrotiriani** —*Virgin of the Cape* and was once isolated. Now it is connected with Sitia by a good road.

From 961-1204 it was only a church, then some cells were added in 1365. The monastery was destroyed by the Turks in 1471 then rebuilt and fortified with a cannon for its protection to deter attackers, thus given the name by the Turks as **"Toplou"** (*Top Cannon ball*). During the Turkish occupation, Toplou became the centre of revolutionaries and a Greek school for children was established to preserve the Greek language and culture.

A plaque on the facade of the chapel has an Hellenistic intristion describing a treaty. The monastery contains a fine collection of icons including one by *Ioannis Cornaros*, a masterpiece from 1770's depicting the Lord — and one by *Frangias Kavertzas* of the Cretan school-16th century. Many other religious relics are in the monastery's collection.

Toplou is a very rich monastery and owns most of the land of the region. It's architecture shows strong Venetian influence. A religious fair takes place on 29 August.

Above left: Moni Toplou — Christ Pantokrator (15th cent). *Above right:* Moni Toplou — The Descend to Death, painted by J. Kornaros (1770). *Below:* Panayia Kera Church — Fresco of the Last Supper.

THE LASITHI COUNTRYSIDE

The District has been divided into two sectors, Western and Eastern, easily identified on the map.

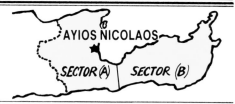

SECTOR (A) — WESTERN LASITHI

(1) Northern Part

SELINARIS MONI *(Monastery)*. This is situated along the main road to Ayios Nikolaos. The chapel is dedicated to St. George. It is customary for local travellers to stop here and pray in the church. The chapel is full of offerings and there is a religious fair on St. George's *(Ayios Yeoryios)* name date, 23 April.

MILATOS CAVE – An ancient site with a cave nearby. In 1823 many Cretans took refuge in the cave to escape from the Turks only to be discovered later and slaughtered.

NEAPOLIS – The central town of the region and the judicial centre of Lasithi district. The inhabitants are well known for their intellectual traditions.

The town has a library and a small collection of antiquities. Pope Alexander V was born near here in 1340 and was called Peter Philargos. It is a rich market place dominated by a modern church.

Tel: Munincipality (0841) 31398
Hospital 32228
KTEL (Bus Company) 32224

PANAYIA KERA-KRITSA

All Holy Lady church is one of the jewels of Byzantine art, the finest church wih frescoes in Crete and dates to the early Venetian period. It has 3 naves with corresponding apses. The Central Nave is dedicated to *VIRGIN MARY*, the North Nave is dedicated to *ST. ANTONY* and the South Nave to *ST. ANNA*, the mother of Mary.

The fascinating frescoes depict various religious scenes including the "Last Supper", "Ayios Yeoryios — the Dragonkiller", "Ayia Anna", "the Massacre of the Innocents" and many others. Although they have been restored, the frescoes retained their original splendour. Being open to the public it is a very popular place to visit.

Nearby is the church of **Ayios Yeoryios Kavoutsis** *(Kavousiotis)* with some interesting wall paintings of the 14th century.

KRITSA VILLAGE – A lovely village built on the side of the hill overlooking the Bay of Mirabello thus providing spectacular views. It is the centre of traditional handicrafts and textiles. Here Jules Dassin directed the film *"Christ Recrucified"*, a novel of the Greek passion written by **Nicos Kazantzakis, called** *"He Who Must Die"*.

LASITHI DISTRICT
(NOMOS LASITHIOU) — 1818 sq. kms
This is the only district of Crete whose "capital" is not of the same name.

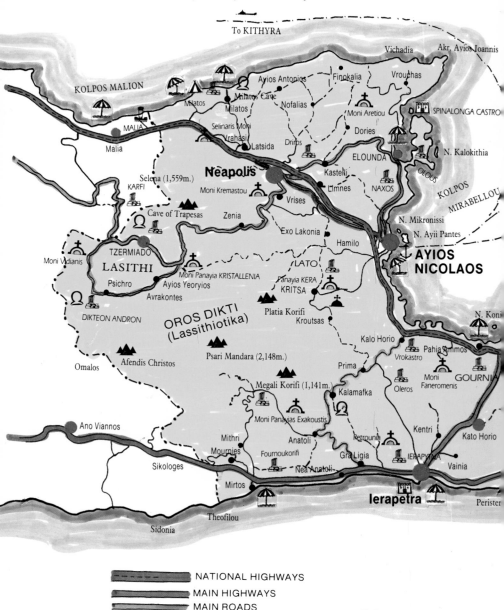

To KITHYRA

Vichadia   Akr. Ayios Joannis

KOLPOS MALION

Ayios Antonies   Finokalia   Vrouchas

Milatos Cave

Milatos   Nofalias

Moni Aretiou   SPINALONGA CASTRO

MALIA

Selinaris Moni

Vrahasi   Latsida   Drims   Dories

Malia

ELOUNDA   N. Kalokithia

Selena (1,559m.)   **Neapolis**   Kasteli

KARFI

Moni Kremastou   Limnes   NAXOS

OLOUS

Cave of Trapesas   Zenia   Vrises

KOLPOS MIRABELLOU

Exo Lakonia   N. Mikronissi

Hamilo   N. Ayii Pantes

Moni Vidianis

TZERMIADO   **AYIOS NICOLAOS**

LASITHI

Psichro   Moni Panayia KRISTALLENIA   LATO

Ayios Yeoryios   Panayia KERA   KRITSA

Avrakontes

DIKTEON ANDRON   Platia Korifi   N. Koni

OROS DIKTI   Kroutsas

(Lassithiotika)

Kalo Horio   Pahia Ammos

Omalos   Afendis Christos   Psari Mandara (2,148m.)   Vrokastro   GOURNIA

Prima   Moni Faneromenis   Oleros

Megali Korifi (1,141m.)   Kalamafka

Ano Viannos   Moni Panayias Exakoustis   Kentri   Kato Horio

Mithri   Anatoli   Retrounia

Mournies   Fournoukorifi   Gra Ligia   IERAPYTNA   Vainia

Sikologes   Nea Anatoli

Mirtos   **Ierapetra**   Perister

Theofilou

Sidonia

NATIONAL HIGHWAYS
MAIN HIGHWAYS
MAIN ROADS
SECONDARY ROADS
FERRY BOAT

N. CHRISSI
(Gaidouronissi)

126   0 1 2   4   8   10 km.

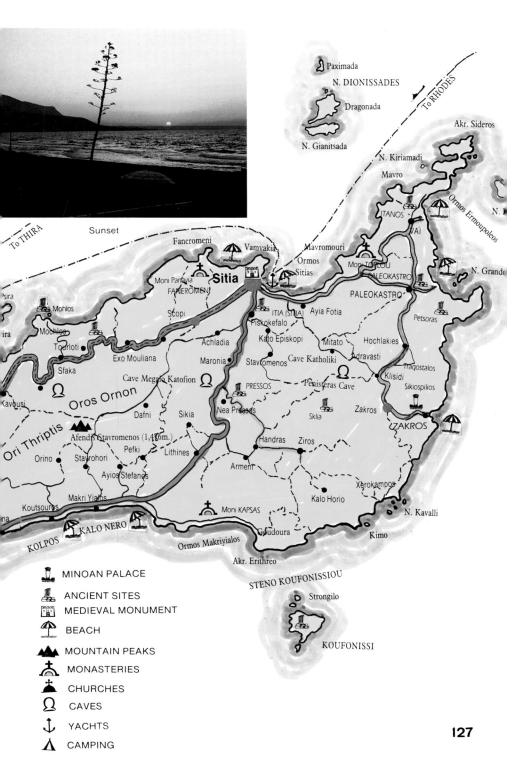

ELOUNDA – Situated to the North of Ayios Nikolaos, it is a major tourist centre with excellent beaches, many hotels and an exclusive tourist complex, the *Elounda Beach Hotel & Bungalows* built in Cretan village style and numerous tavernas — Sea sports facilities are available.

Elounda is protected by the **Spinalonga Peninsula** and under the Venetians it became a trading port. At the Isthmus where the land is connected to Spinalonga Peninsula with a small bridge, there are abandoned windmills and the dykes, with salt flats, were producing salt until recently.

Elounda has been used as a centre of filming various television series including the "Lotus Eaters". Tel: Police (0841)...... ... 41348

SPINALONGA ISLAND – a small islet to the north of Spinalonga peninsula with a most impressive Venetian Fortress which was built in 1579 after the Fort of Ayios Nikolaos was abandoned. It was one of the last outspots of the Venetians and finally surrendered to the Turks in 1715 who held it up to 1903. It then became a leper colony which was eventually cleared and cleaned. Now it is a tourist attraction and visitors come by boat either from Elounda or Ayios Nikolaos.

Windmills at the Isthmus which joins Elounda and the area of the ancient site of Olous.

the island of Spinalonga and Castle.

Above: General view of the idyllic harbour of Elounda; a picturesque and relaxing resort.
Below: The Spinalonga Bay in the early morning mist.

PAHIA AMMOS – A small harbour near **Gournia, perhaps was its ancient harbour. Some Minoan tombs with trussed bodies were found jammed into burial jars** *(the same type of burials were found at Pyrgos).* The modern village provides hotel accommodation and good beaches.

VASILIKI – A Minoan settlement to the south of Gournia *(see archaeological sites)* and close to the modern village of Vasiliki. It dates to circa 2500BC but very little remain although some extraordinary pottery of red and black colours was found here, similar to pottery found in other Mediterranean places but this is of a superior quality. They are on display at Heraklion Museum — Case 6. There are also signs of a Roman presence.

IERAPETRA

The main centre to the south and the biggest town along the whole south coast of Crete. It has a harbour and a long sandy beach along which are numerous tavernas and cafeterias. The town attracts many visitors and has some good hotels.

It is an agricultural centre and due to its very mild climate it provides winter crops of tomatoes, cucumbers and other vegetables which are exported to mainland Greece and Europe. Ierapetra also produces very fine wine.

Situated on the site of ancient **IERAPITNA** (westernside of the town) was a trading harbour for traffic between Crete, Africa and Asia and was the last Cretan city to fall into Roman hands. It flourished under the Romans as a port and the ruins of fine buildings, including a theatre, were found. There is a **Venetian fort** which originally was built by the Genoese in the early 13th century AD; a Minaret and a Fountain from the Turkish period are in the old town to the south west. It was said that Napoleon stayed here overnight on his way to Egypt.

Ierapetra with its long beach.

Above Top: Part of the walls of the Venetian Fort of Ierapetra. *Above:* A church tower at Ierapetra-old town.

In the town there is a Library and a small **museum** with Minoan and other exhibits including interesting sargophagii found at Vasiliki.

Tel: Muninicipality (0842) 22246
     KTEL (Bus Services)............... 28237
     Hospital............................... 22252
     Harbour Authorities 22294
     Police................................. 22560

GAIDOURONISSI –
A small island just to the south of Ierapetra with an unusually coloured beach. It can be reached by boat.

MIRTOS –
is to the west of Ierapetra with some Minoan remains. There is a strong evidence of the manufacture of textiles and pottery. The modern village close to the ancient site was destroyed by the Germans in 1943 and most of its inhabitants were killed. It was rebuilt after the war and it is now a small tourist resort, discovered originally by the hippies in the 1960's. It has limited hotel accommodation but has fine beaches.

PYRGOS –
About ½ mile from Mirtos, it is a hilltop Minoan village only recently excavated (work continues) and although most was destroyed, it has brought to light evidence of the astonishing richness of provincial Crete during the Minoan period.

131

LASITHI PLAIN

This is the most important inland place to visit in Crete. A natural beauty spot, a unique place of its own, some 6-8 kms long and 4-6 kms wide, surrounded by high mountains and it is well known for the thousands of its windmills; many are neglected unfortunately, but others are still in use and when they are in full white sails, they are a magnificent sight.

If you come from the north, from Heraklion via Hersonissos you reach the peak passage with an enormous drop to the west, at *Ambelos Afhim* where the remains of many windmills can be seen. From the Tourist Cafe (6) you see the Panoramic view of the plain.

There are about 21 villages small and large at the edges and foothills some very rich and some abandoned. A unique place, it was established in ancient times and finds of all periods of history have been unearthed however, none of great importance.

The Venetians alarmed by the Independent spirit of the people, removed most of the inhabitants and prohibited any kind of farming from 1362 to the 15th century. Eventually they lost the struggle and the people were allowed back.

TZERMIADES
to the northeast is the largest village, a rich agricultural centre with a small hotel and guest houses. Close by is the cave of **TRAPEZA** where interesting finds were discovered dating to the Neolithic period including Pro-Minoan burials and a Minoan cult shrine. Tel: Police (0844) 22208

MONI PANAYIA KRISTALLENIA
built on a rocky hill, the monastery was destroyed twice by the Turks for its revolutionary activities *(see monasteries).*

PSIHRO,
to the southwestern side, is the agricultural centre of this region with some accommodation. On the side of the hill there is an observation post with a tourist pavilion (5) from where there are excellent views of the plain. Tel: Police (0844)... 31292

DIKTEO ANDRO –
A cave to the west of Psihro reached only on foot. Guides with mules are always available and a guide is advisable, if you wish to explore the inside of the cave as it can be slippery. Protective clothing and suitable shoes are essential for detailed exploration. The interior of the cave is beautiful with stalagmites and stalaktites, including a large one in the depth of the cave. There are some remains from the Middle Minoan to the Archaic periods and some table stones for offerings were found including one with Linear A writing which is at Oxford.

Lasithi Plain is an agricultural centre, producing oranges, apples, pears, potatoes and vegetables and is well watered.

SUMMIT OF MT. DIKTYS –
2,148 metres (7045 feet). Explorers and hikers will enjoy fascinating views of most of the eastern region of Crete and can observe the butterflies, birds and flowers. However, only experienced hikers should attempt such a trek as Cretan mountains can be unfriendly and extremely dangerous.

A view of Lasithi Plain.

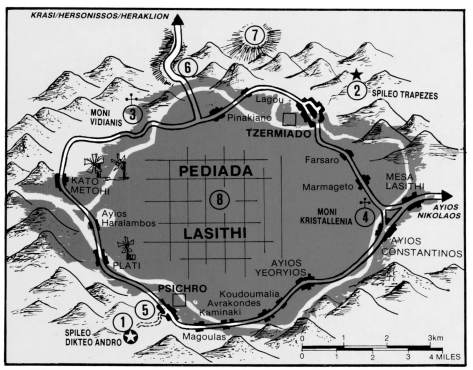

MYTHOLOGY

Kronos, the master of earth, feared to be overthrown by his children and ate them all. When his wife Rhea bore the latest child *Zeus,* to protect him, she gave a stone to Kronos instead of Zeus. The baby was given to the Kouretes to conceal in the cave and was looked after by the goat "Amaltheia" and the bee "Melissa". In order that Kronos should not hear the baby's cries, the Kouretes beat their shields.

(1) DIKTEO ANDRO CAVE
(2) TRAPEZES CAVE
(3) VIDIANIS MONASTERY
(4) KRISTALLENIA MONASTERY
(5) TOURIST PAVILION (offers panoramic views of Lasithi)
(6) TOURIST SPOT with remains of Windmills — offers panoramic views of Lasithi)
(7) KARFI Ancient Settlement (see under Heraklion district)
(8) Remains of VENETIAN DRAINAGE WORKS

General view of Lasithi Plain in the Spring (H. Panteris)

SECTOR (B) — EASTERN SIDE

PSIRA ISLAND – Opposite Ayios Nikolaos to the east, 3km offshore north of Mokhlos is 2½km long. The island was a settlement and port in ancient times and finds indicate close links with Egypt, Syria and Palestine.

MOKHLOS – A circular mass of land 200 metres offshore. The modern village is on the other side on land. An ancient city with tombs existed here and vases, marble and sealstones were found.

THE NORTHERN COAST – is very picturesque and the road between KAVOUSI and SITIA provide excellent views of the coastline. It is called the *"Cretan Riviera"* and goes through the villages of **Platanos, Sfakia, Exo Mouliana.**

KHAMEZI – An ancient settlement with remains of an oval structure of the proto-palatian Minoan period. The only known structure of its type and it is believed that it was a sort of a sanctuary.

SITIA

A picturesque town built amphitheatrically over the gulf and the harbour is full of caiques and fishing boats; it is visited infrequently by ships and there is a weekly service connecting Rhodes with Ayios Nikolaos and Pireaus. To the eastern side of the town there is an excellent beach and the area has many Hotels and Apartments. Tavernas provide delicious food and excellent fish. It is an ideal tourist centre for the exploration of the surrounding areas and bus services connect it regularly with Ayios Nikolaos Heraklion and Ierapetra. In the summer, special bus connections reach Toplou monastery and Vai beach.

The region was known to be the home of ancient **ETEOCRETANS** the true post Minoan Cretans. After the destruction of the Minoan civilisation many Minoan Cretans came to settle in these areas, around Sitia and further to the south, up to Pressos *(see archaeological sites).* Ancient Sitia was called **ITIS** or **ITIA** and was on the eastern side of the bay, about 1km away from modern Sitia in an area called *Petra Hill.* Many of the ancient buildings were discovered recently but nothing much is known of its antiquity.

Modern Sitia was established by the Venetians with a harbour and a castle of which very little remains. In 1362 natives and Venetians rebelled and by joining forces declared an Independent Demograce of St. Titos. In 1538 the town was besieged by the pirate Barbarossa who failed to occupy it. Under the Turks it declined but now has expanded not only as the centre of the region but also as an attractive tourist resort.

Here was born one of the most famous Cretans, **KORNAROS,** the author of the famous medieval masterpiece *EROTOKRITOS,* a poem of 10,000 lines, of a love story between Erotokritos, son of Pesestratos and Aretousa, daughter of the Athenian King Hercules. An annual event of cultural events, folklore and music takes place every summer called KORNARIA.

There is a small collection of Folk Art, **Laographic Museum** with embroideries, weaving, handicraft, costumes, icons etc.

Tel: Muninicipality (0843) 28204
Hospital............................. 22231
Harbour Authorities 22310
Police................................ 22266
KTEL (Bus Services).............. 22272

Old picture of Sitia from the collection of H. Panteris.

134

Above: General view of Sitia. *Below:* The picturesque village of Riskokefalo, south of Sitia.

RISKOKEFALO – To the south of Sitia, was a Minoan site with a sanctuary on the peak where many small motive statuettes were found.

ZOU – Further south has a Minoan farmhouse which is preserved in a fair condition and is situated some 300 metres to the north of the village. From this spot you can enjoy very good views of the coastline to the north.

AYIA FOTIA – To the east of Sitia, this is an early and extensive Minoan cemetery where around 250 tombs were discovered. Finds include copper daggers, hundreds of vases, a box containing gold etc. Most of the finds are at Ayios Nikolaos Museum.

VAI – To the north eastern part of the coast, this is an idyllic and very romantic place, unique of its kind, with tropical atmosphere, due to the many palm trees, along the valley and by the sandy bay where there are cafes providing food and refreshments. The fine beach and the beauty of the place attracts many people during the summer and some people camp in tents amongst the palm trees.

To the north is ancient **ITANOS** *(see archaeological sites)* with excellent views and coves with sandy beaches.

Above and below: Two scenes of Vai Bay which resembles Carribean resorts.

ISLANDS – To the north are three isolated and uninhabited islands: **DIONISSADES ISLANDS** — **Paximadia** *(dry biscuits)* to the north with a lighthouse, **Dragonara** (the biggest) in the middle and **Gianissada.** They can be reached by boat from Sitia.

East of Itanos is **Elassa** island 2½kms long with a grey limestone flat top.

PALEOKASTRO – A modern village along the eastern coast with tourist complexes and apartments amongst olive groves. The bay provides fine beaches and this isolated area is popular with young people who prefer the simple type of holidays.

In the surrounding areas, closer to the sea, are the scattered remains of the ancient **Paleokastro.** It was a harbour from the Minoan to Hellenistic periods although nothing dramatic has been discovered, except a small Minoan palace, the only one to be rebuilt after the great catastrophe of 1450BC.

ANO ZAKROS – This is the centre of the eastern region and provides some hotel accommodation and is well known for the fine spring water. The land is very fertile. To the south east is Kato Zakros *(see ancient sites)* and between the two there is a deep gorge called *"Valley of the Dead"* where many Minoan burials were discovered.

SOUTH EAST COAST – Like the south western coast of Crete, this region is also isolated and can be explored much easier by boat than by car.

SOUTH COAST – East of Ierapetra. The good road between Ierapetra and the Bay of **Kalo Nero** the village of **Analipsi** goes through beaches, olive groves, inland mountains, gorges and bays with beaches, most popular that of **Makris Yialos,** and isolated hotels.

KOUFONISSI *(light or deaf island)*, off the south east coast. It is an island with small islet peaks to the north and south. It was an ancient settlement and recent excavations revealed amongst other things a theatre with 10 rows of seats.

Above: The idyllic Agathia Beach near Paleokastro village.
Below left: The sandy beach of Makri Yialos east of Ierapetra.

BEACHES OF THE DISTRICT

Within the town of Ayios Nicolaos there is a very small, mainly pebbled beach by the main bus stop. However, a few kms to the south near Istro, 12 kms, is the beautiful beach of Vailisma. Further south is the bay of Pahia Amnos. To the North is the fine beach of Elounda with one of the biggest hotel complexes in Crete.

Sitia, Vai and **Paleokastro** also provide excellent beaches so is **Ierapetra** and the surrounding coast.

ACCOMMODATION

Hotel accommodation is plentiful but mainly concentrated in the area of Ayios Nicolaos and Elounda. Sitia and Ierapetra also have all types of hotel accommodation. For a complete list of all types of accommodation please contact the local National Tourist Organisation of Greece, the Association of Cretan Hoteliers, Malikouti Street — Heraklion or the Munincipality of Ayios Nikolaos — Tel. 28286

CAMPING:

AYIOS NICOLAOS: Gournia Moun. Tel: (0841) — Up to 160 people; by the beach.

IERAPETRA: Tel: (0842) 61351. Around 120 people; by the beach.

KOUTSOUNARI: Tel: (0842) 61213 and 190 people; by the beach.

ENTERTAINMENT

Apart from local festivals and folklore events, entertainment in this area is geared mainly for the young where the main tourist centres provide numerous discotheques. However the numerous tavernas provide an exciting evening out. During the summer there is a small number of Greek clubs both in Ayios Nikolaos and Elounda, worth visiting.

TRAVELLING AROUND

Communications in the region mainly between all the main centres, tourist areas and archaeological sites have been lately improved and roads are in very good condition. All the major centres are also connected by regular bus service.

BUS STATIONS

Ayios Nicolaos: Atlantidos Sq. .... Tel. 28284
Ierapetra: G. Giananaka St. 28237
Sitia: A. Papanastasiou St. 28272

Ayios Nikolaos is connected with Heraklion through a regular service. Regular bus services also connect Ierapetra, Elounda, Kritsa, Lasithi, Gournia, Sitia and Vai.

SITIA has a small airport and flights connect it with Heraklion. Also with Rhodes and Karpathos Island.

OLYMPIC AIRWAYS-Sitia 22270
Airport: (0843) 24666

USEFUL ADDRESSES —

AYIOS NICOLAOS (Other areas stated)

	(0841)
TOURIST INFORMATION OFFICE, by the Lake	Tel. 22276
TOURIST POLICE by the Lake	22321
Police at Ierapetra	22560
Police at Sitia	22266
POST OFFICE by the Lake	22099
TELEPHONES (OTE) by the Lake	22099
OLYMPIC AIRWAYS — Koundourou St.	22033
HARBOUR AUTHORITY by the harbour	22312
Munincipality	28286
Archaeological Museum	22462
Banks: General Bank	23414
National Bank	28855
Bank of Greece	28446
Commercial Bank	22779
Bank of Crete	23730
ANEK-Steamship — Ayios Nicolaos	28114
Sitia	28466
STATE HOSPITAL — Ayios Nicolaos	22369
Neapolis	32228
Ierapetra	22252
Sitia	22231
EMERGENCIES	100

Note: Every effort has been made to provide accurate information but we do not take responsibility for any changes or omissions.

FESTIVALS — EVENTS

LATO Festival — Ayios Nicolaos in July. Musical events, ballet, theatre etc. of Greece and Europe. An excellent festival.

Dekapentavgoustos at Neapoli 14-15 August. Religious and popular events.

KRITSIA — during August. Events include a traditional Cretan wedding.

Mesokampits — Events during 28-29 August in all Lasithi.

Sultana Festival — Sitia 2nd part of August 3-5 days.

KORNARIA — Sitia during August. Folklore events in memory of the Cretan poet Kornaros.

Kazanemata — Pisko Kefalo near Sitia. Middle of September. Traditional way of producing RAKI, the traditional strong Cretan drink. Excellent eating too.

KYRVIA — at Ierapetra in July. Cultural and folklore events.

People dancing at a local festival.

A general view of one of Crete's most picturesque bays — Vai Bay in late afternoon.

GEOGRAPHICAL INTRODUCTION

GEOGRAPHY

Crete is situated almost in the centre of the Mediterranean basin. To the west it is about 100km (61 miles) from southern Peloponese. It is some 260km (160 miles) long and in width varies from 60km (36 miles) to 12km (7.5 miles). Its overall size is 8,280 square kms (3,200 sq. miles).

Under the Venetians, the northern coast (western part) was the centre of the sea routes from Venice to Crete coming down along the Peloponese coast, however all links with the west stopped under the Turks and one could reach Crete only from the eastern ports of Syria, Smyrna and Constantinople.

The Cretan mountains give a special character to the island, the remains of a once continuous arc of folds which stretched from the Peloponese to Crete and Asia Minor.

CLIMATE

The climate is variable; from sub-tropical to sub-alpine. Thus distinctive zones exist with their own types of natural vegetation.

THE COAST: It is generally mild but some southern parts have near tropical temperatures. However, the months of November, December, January, February and early March are fairly cold with temperatures dropping to below 14°C (58°F). However the wind can be cold, especially on the northern coast.

The rainfall is very small and non existent in the summer. When it does come, the rain is torrential with thunderstorms; but even during the winter months there are long periods of sunshine. While snow-bound mountain peaks disappear into the sky, some southern coastal places can be warm. Temperatures gradually increase as the summer approaches its maximum in July and August with everlasting sunshine, clear blue skies and temperatures to the 80's.

THE HILLS: These are generally situated between the coastal plain and the mountain peaks and cover most of the area of Crete, roughly about ⅔, and heights are up to 800m (2626F). Temperatures are slightly lower than those by the coast and there is frost during winter months. Rainfall can occur during the months of October to May.

HIGH MOUNTAINS: These are dominant mountain peaks over 800m and in contrast to the coast, provide cool temperatures and much more rain. Snow covers most of the highest peaks in January, February even early March and in severe winters they become difficult to reach. Most of Crete's mountains are rocky and barren.

TEMPERATURES: These are average temperatures and at places can be much warmer in the summer or colder in the winter.

	F	°C		F	°C
JAN	54	12	JUL	78	26
FEB	54	12	AUG	78	26
MAR	57	14	SEPT	75	24
APR	62	17	OCT	69	21
MAY	68	20	NOV	63	17
JUNE	74	23	DEC	58	14

PLANTS & CULTIVATION

COASTS: The coastal plains which are very narrow in places, are the richest and most fertile. Intensive cultivation in some areas provides double cropping and farmland is highly prized.

PLANTS include the **Mastic Bush** (*pistacia lentiscus*) — a small 3 metres high plant with characteristics such as resinous smell, red berries which are blackened gradually during the summer, and **Carob Tree** — a tree well adapted to surviving in long periods of drought, even in poor, rocky soil.

Above: A typical Cretan landscape with Olive groves. *Right:* Cretan vineyards are very well looked after.

Common to the coast is **Algrave** *(century plant)*, an enormous cactus-like plant of bluish green leaves growing up to 2 metres long with sharp spines along their edges; this is also a native to Mexico. The flower-stern grows fast, up to a height of 10 metres in a month and after flowering it dries. Aromatic plants include **Thyme** and flowering shrubs include **Rock Roses**.

Palm Trees were brought by the Arabs and flourish in some sheltered areas; the most well known is around VAI.

Bananas are cultivated extensively around Mallia, **Oranges** grow in the Hania region and **Peanuts** in Rethymno. **Tomatoes** and **Vegetables** are grown in the Messara valley and Ierapetra area.

HILL ZONES: Crete was once covered in forest but gradually it was destroyed for various reasons including the use of wood for fuel; also there are over a million sheep and goats which inflicted further damage.

No serious effort has been made yet for forestry planning except in some areas, so you will see naked hills and mountains, interesting mainly to the geologists.

However, other places are covered by vast numbers of **Olive trees**, some well looked after, as olives and olive oil are a major agricultural product. There are estimated 16-18 million olive trees in Crete.

Vineyards occupy many hill sides and valleys. Summer is the busy time of harvesting. Some grapes are turned into wine, some into sultanas and others are table grapes. **Almond trees** provide a good income and require little attention. **Carrob trees** can also be found.

The making of Sultanas — Grapes drying in the sun.

There are over 100 different flowers including **Narcissus, Anemones, Orchids, Iris, Prickly Pears.**

The hills with bright **Yellow Gorse**, blankets of **Daisies** and **Poppies** are a delight in the spring. In the summer are **Jasmine** with its sweet smell, **Honey Suckle, Oleander** and flowering **Thyme** which gives the special aromatic taste used in honey. **Cyclamen** also grow wild.

MOUNTAIN ZONE: Where you find trees, **Pine** is the most common and they are usually found in the southern part of Crete. **Cypress** trees are impressive, some can reach 20 metres (66 feet) height. **Ilex, Chestnuts** and **Planes** to be found in some places, as well as in the hilly areas.

There is no plant life cultivated in the mountains, only sheep grazing.

Flowers include **Anemone, Cyclamen, Daphne, Tulips, Yellow Eyed Crocus, Glory of the Snow.**

FAUNA

The **Donkey** is still in use in the village, and together with the **Mule** was until recently the only means of land communication and travel. Horses are not common in Crete.

AGRINI *(Kri-Kri)* also known as *Wild Ibex*. It is a type of goat with horns. Where shown in Minoan art, they are now to be found in some parts of the mountains and are well protected.

BIRDS: There is a large variety of beautiful birds, permanently in Crete, including **Warblers, Jarks, Goldfingers, Falcons, Eagles** and some **Vulture.** Crete is also on the route of many migrating birds including **Swallows, Hoopers** and **Bee eaters.**

GENERAL INFORMATION

GREEK NATIONAL TOURIST ORGANISATION (G.N.T.O.)

CRETE MAIN OFFICE: 1 Xanthouolidou Street (opposite Museum) Tel. (081) 222 487/8 HERAKLION

GREEK HEAD OFFICE: 2 Amerikis Street. ATHENS Tel. (01) 32231

G.N.T.O. OFFICES ABROAD

AUSTRALIA: 51-57 Pitt Str. Sydney
Also for N.S.W 2000
New Tel. 241 16 63
Zealand

AUSTRIA: Kärntner Ring 5, 1015 Wien Tel. 525.317

BELGIUM: 62-66 Blv. de l'Impératrice, 1000-Bruxelles, Tel. 513 02 06

CANADA: a) 1233 de la Montagne,Montreal Q.C. Quebec H3G 1Z2. Tel. 871 15 35.
b) 80 Bloor Str. West, Suite 1403, Toronto ONT M5S 2V1, Tel. 968 22 20

DENMARK: Vester Farimagsyade 3, DK 1606 Köpenhagen, Tel. 1-123 063

FINLAND: Stora Robertsgatan 3-5C 38, 00120 Helsingfors 12, Tel. 0-655 223

FRANCE: 3 Avenue de l'Opera, Paris 75001 Tel. 260 65 75

W. GERMANY: a) Neue Mainzerstr. 22, 6 Frankfurt/Main 1, Tel. 236 562
b) Pacellistr. 2, 8000 München 2, Tel. 222 035
c) Neuer Wall 35, 2000 Hamburg 36, Tel. 366 910

ITALY: a) Via L. Bissolati 78-80, 00187 Roma, Tel. 474 43 01
b) Piazza Diaz 1, Ang. Via Rastrelli, Milan Tel. 860470

JAPAN: 3-16-30 Nishi Azabu, Minato-Ku, Tokyo 10 Tel. 403 18 12

NETHERLANDS: Leidsestraat 13, NS Amsterdam Tel. 254212

NORWAY: Ovre Slottsgatan 15B, Oslo 1, Tel. 42650

SAUDIA ARABIA: Embassy of Greece, Madin Road, City Centre, PO Box 13262, Jedda 21493, Tel. 667 6240

SPAIN: C/Allerto Aquilera No. 17, Madrid, Tel. 248 4889

SWEDEN: Grev Turegatan 2, Box 5298, 1024 Stockholm 5, Tel. 203 802

SWITZERLAND: Gottfried Kellerstr. 7, CH 800 Zürich, Tel. 251 8487

UNITED KINGDOM: 195-197 Regent St. London W1R 8DL, Tel. 734 5997
Also for Ireland

U.S.A. a) 645 Fifth Aven. Olympic Tower, New York N.Y. 10022, Tel. 421 5777
b) 611 West Sixth Str., Los Angeles California 90017, Tel. 626 6696
c) 168 North Michigan Ave. Chicago Illinois 60601, Tel. 782 1084
d) Building 31, State Str. Boston Mas 02109, Tel. 227 7366

For countries not mentioned above, please contact th Greek Embassy which may be able to assist.

TOURIST POLICE IN CRETE
HERAKLION: Dikeosinis Street, Tel. (081) 28319
HANIA: 42 Karaiskakis Street, Tel. (0821) 24477
AYIOS NICOLAOS: 7 Omirou St, Tel. (0841) 2232
RETHYMNO: 214 Arkadiou Str., Tel. (0831) 2815

HOW TO GET TO CRETE

BY AIR: There are direct charter flights from most European countries, mainly to Heraklion but these are organised for all inclusive holidays, although seats are sold separately subject to availability.

Otherwise you can travel to either Heraklio or Hania via Athens. OLYMPIC AIRWAYS has regular daily flights from Athens to Heraklion (*3-9 flights daily according to season*) and to Hania 3-5 flights daily.

There are about 4-7 flights weekly to and from Rhodes and during the summer there are som flights between Santorini and Heraklion.

BY BOAT: Regular passenger and car ferrie connect Crete with the main Greek port o PIRAEUS and also other places.

PIRAEUS-HERAKLION - Daily departure every evening from Piraeus arrive at Heraklio in the early hours of the morning; it take about 12 hours. Organised by MINOAN LINES.

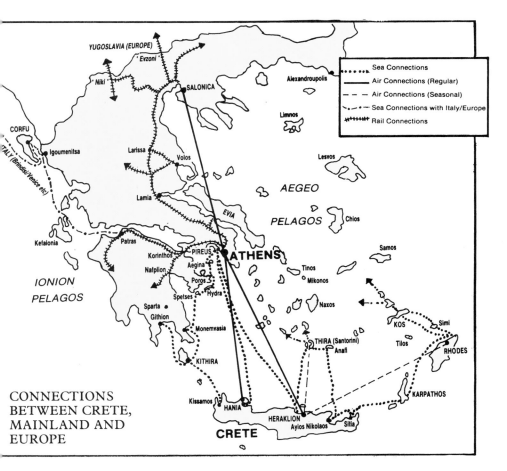

**CONNECTIONS
BETWEEN CRETE,
MAINLAND AND
EUROPE**

PIRAEUS-HANIA — Daily departures every evening from Piraeus arrive at Souda Bay in the early hours of the morning; it takes about 11 hours. Organised by ANEK LINES.

Both lines offer comfortable boats from expensive cabins to cheap tourist class. Extra services are added in the summer months.

PIRAEUS-CRETE-RHODES — A weekly round trip between Piraeus-Ayios Nikolaos-Sitia-Karpathos Island-Rhodes. Times are less regular depending on weather conditions.

PIRAEUS-PELOPONESE-CRETE — A weekly service from Piraeus-Monenvasia-Neapolis *(both in the eastern Peloponese)* Kithyra Island and Kastelli Kissamou *(Western Crete).* Ideal for those who enjoy a sea voyage.

SANTORINI-HERAKLION – A regular daily service during the tourist period from Heraklio to the volcanic island of Santorini *(Thyra)* which is about 100km north of Crete. The service is widely used for daily excursions for groups or individuals.

PASSENGER LINERS and CAR FERRIES connecting various eastern Mediterranean ports from VENICE-ANCONA or BRINDISSI *(Italy)* DUBROVNIK *(Yugoslavia),* PATRAS, CORFU, PIRAEUS, RHODES *(Greece),* LIMASSOL, LARNACA *(Cyprus),* ALEXANDRIA and HAIFA.

The major lines operating such services include: SOL, ANDRIATICA, MEDITERRANEAN SUN LINES, EPIROTIKI LINES, KAVOUNIDES LINES, MARITIME Co. of LESVOS, STABILITY LINES.

Cruise ships stop at Heraklion and trips to Knossos and other places are organised.

BY RAIL: You may travel to Crete by rail through Europe to Athens-Piraeus and from there by boat to Crete, although you will appreciate that it is time consuming but an inexpensive way to travel.

Further information can be obtained from HELLENIC RAILWAYS 1-3 Karaolou Street-Athens.

143

BY CAR: For those taking their car, the best way is to get a ferry boat from the most convenient port of your own country or to travel all the way to Piraeus.

For Common Market citizens a valid driving licence is required and the same applies to Canadian and U.S. citizens. Other visitors require an international driving licence. Take with you the registration of your car (log book) and your insurance card.

If you are a member of an Automobile Association they will supply you with further information and inform you about the Greek Automobile Association **ELPA,** or you may contact them directly:

Athens: 2-4 Messogiou St., or 6 Amerikis St.
Heraklion: Knossos Avenue Tel. (081) 289440
Hania: Apokoronou Street

TOUR OPERATORS: Still the most popular way to arrange your holidays. Just visit your local travel agent or tour operator and select the place and time and the rest will be arranged for you. The Greek Tourist Office in your country will supply you with a list of tour operators featuring Crete.

PASSPORTS

To enter both Greece and Crete it is important to have a valid passport. For Common Market Nationals, formalities are much simpler. No visa is required for most countries except those with which Greece has no formal agreements.

Citizens of the Common Market are subject to the Communitie's agreements for long stays. Citizens of Austria, Canada, New Zealand, Cyprus and some others can stay for 3 months, (U.S. citizens for 2 months) and you apply to the local police for extension if required.

CUSTOMS

Those visitors entering Crete directly, are subject to normal custom controls and regulations. Those entering via Athens *(by air)* are subject to custom controls there. Their flight to Crete is internal and no further custom controls will apply at Hania or Heraklion. On the return journey the same applies.

Those travelling by boat, the same formalities apply. The first place of arrival is subject to customs controls.

CAR CONTROLS — When entering, the customs will stamp your passport and note the number of your vehicle. This gives you free entry lasting 4 months, with further extension after you apply at Heraklion Custom's offices. If you enter Crete via other Greek ports or frontiers, formalities will apply at the first place of entry.

If you decide to sell the car, you must comply with customs regulations including local taxes, registration etc.

CURRENCY-BANKS

You are allowed a limited amount of drahmas to taken in from abroad although there is no limitati of travellers cheques or cash amounts. If howev you take cash exceeding £300 or US $500 appr must be declared. Exchange rates fluctuate acc ding to local or International factors. Travelle cheques can be exchanged in all Banks and lar organisations. Most internationally-used cre cards can also be used but only in some places.

Banks can exchange most foreign money. They open daily (Monday-Friday) 8.30am-1pm. tourist areas extended hours and weekend openi are common in order that the best service is given visitors. The currency unit in Greece since ancie times is the **DRAHMA.** 2 Drahma = 100 Lepta *Bank Notes:* 50, 100, 500, 1000, 5000 drahmas *Coins:* 1, 2, 5, 10, 20 drahmas.

HEALTH

All major towns and some large villages ha hospitals, with the fullest range of medical nee concentrated in Heraklion. Hospitals treat patier free in contrast to Doctor's clinics which are priva as are the dentists. Chemist shops are to be found most places and will provide medicine but do not surprised at the high prices.

People unused to changes of climate, heat or forei food may suffer from gastritis. Do not panic, apart from some discomfort, it is common. You c get the appropriate tablets from your local chemis or you may use lots of lemon juice (no sugar) wi soda water to wash out the system.

Drinking water is clean but if you are worried y can buy bottled water which is plentiful. Note: d to the lack of rain in the summer months, water very precious so do not waste it in any way.

Toilets in general are good. Public toilets are us by many people from different countries wi different habits which may not be of your liking. is advisable that you carry with you toilet paper hand wipers.

ACCOMMODATION

HOTELS — Hotel accommodation in Crete plentiful and is concentrated in the towns and all tourist areas; everyone is catered for.

Services vary and depend on the type of ho and its purpose. For instance, many hotels town centres are generally old, noisy *(due to t traffic)* and lack parking space. Others may n offer all the services expected.

The categories of the hotels are:

DE LUXE: Expensive but very good.

CLASS A: Vary, according to age and location b generally good and expensive.

CLASS B & C: Offer more standard facilities, mo with private bathroom/wc.

CLASS D & E: Much lower standards but inexpe sive for those who prefer simpler accommodatior

FURNISHED APARTMENTS/VILLAS

— These are mainly new with local architectural character, some in larger complexes with many facilities including cafeteria or taverna and swimming pool; ideal for families. They provide bedroom(s), dining-lounge, kitchen with fridge and cooking facilities, bathroom and toilet.

An up-to-date list of Hotels and Apartments in Crete can be obtained from the Greek Tourist Organisation.

Another booklet which also contains a list of travel agents and tour operators in Crete can be obtained from the ASSOCIATION OF CRETAN HOTEL-IERS, Idomeneos and Malikouti Street-Heraklion. Tel. (081) 223 967 Telex: 262380.

PENSIONS-GUESTHOUSES-TAVER-NAS

— There is extensive accommodation of this type in tourist areas. Some provide good facilities including private bathroom or shower. But others offer just a simple room accommodation. They are ideal for those on excursions for short stays.

YOUTH HOSTELS

— These are open to all members of the International Youth Hostels Association and for further information you may write to the GREEK YOUTH HOSTEL ASSOCIATION, 4 Dragatsaniou Street, Glaftonos Sq. Athens, Y.W.C.A. in Rethymno-Timios Stavros Quarter - Tel. (0831) 23324.

CAMPING

— There are several camping sites in Crete and most are listed in the district sections, or contact the Greek National Tourist Organisation for a leaflet.

GENERAL SERVICES

POSTAL — Postal services connect Crete with the rest of the world mainly with air mail service. Stamps can be obtained from all post offices or kiosks. Different rates apply to different countries, although for postcards, rates are cheaper. The same rates apply to all mail sent to other parts of Crete or all over Crete.

Registered letters must not be sealed as the attendant may demand to check the contents.

TELEPHONES/TELEGRAMS — Crete is connected directly with Europe and most other countries. Direct coding numbers can be obtained from most hotels or the local tele-communications office.

If you have no access to a telephone, the Greek Telecommunication Organisation OTE has offices in all towns and main tourist centres and an attendant will help you to dial your country from a telephone box and then pay according to the time used. This is a cheaper way to ring abroad as hotels charge extra for service.

Telegrams can be sent everywhere from the above mentioned offices.

GENERAL NOTES

ELECTRICITY — The normal (standard) electricity supply throughout Greece is 220 volts AC. A two pin continental adaptor is required.

TIME — Greece and Crete is in the Eastern European time zone which is 2 hours ahead of Greenwich Mean Time. Summer is from April to September.

WEIGHTS – 1 kilo (1000 grammes) = 2.2lb
½ kilo = 1.1lb
¼ kilo = ½lb approx.
1 litre (dry) = 0.9 quart
1 litre (liquid) = 1.06 quarts approx.

PETROL: This is served in litres from petrol filling stations and prices are average as in Europe. They fluctuate according to international trends.
Distances: 1 square kilometer = 0.39 sq. mile
1 mile = 1.5km approx.
1 hectar = 2.47 acres.

The weights and measures generally follow the French metric system although they are now adapting to the Common Market.

TIPPING — *Hotels* charge a 10-15% service charge which is included in the bill. A porter who will take your luggage to your room (many do not do that) and a chambermaid usually welcome something.

Restaurants usually add a service charge on the bill but it is customary to leave behind some drahmas.

Taxis. It is customary to give a few drahmas but you can do without if you so wish.

Hairdressing – some tipping is expected.

NEWSPAPERS/BOOKS — Mainly English, German, French or Italian language newspapers, magazines and paperbacks can be obtained from newsagents which are mainly the kiosks. Foreign newspapers are normally one day behind.

MUSEUMS and ARCHAEOLOGICAL SITES

Crete is famous for the Heraklion Museum which houses the richest collection from the MINOAN Civilisation. There are many important archaeological sites, the best known of all is KNOSSOS.

MUSEUMS — They open early in the morning to late afternoon with a short break between 1-3pm. During the winter months they open later and close earlier but remain open all day.

During Sundays and Bank Holidays opening hours are shorter. Most museums close once a week but the closing day varies from Museum to Museum, so it is better to enquire from your hotel or tourist office.

There is an entrance fee to all visitors except students of Archaeology, Greek Nationals and a few others.

Photography is usually allowed in most museums but in some places you may have to pay extra. The use of a flash or tripod is forbidden unless a permit is obtained.

ARCHAEOLOGICAL SITES

They open around 8-9am till sunset, with shorter hours for Sundays and holidays. There is an entrance fee to all except as shown above. Photography is usually allowed except where signs indicate otherwise. This applies to newly excavated areas.

Both museums and archaeological sites are closed on January 1st, March 25th, Easter Holidays and Christmas.

SMALL CHURCHES & SMALL SITES

These are usually locked. An inquiry at the nearest Kafenio or police station will lead to the keeper who will be glad to assist you.

ANTIQUITIES

These are important both to the Cretan inheritance and to visitors like you, who wish to admire them, so when you visit archaeological sites, please do not climb over walls or pillars, do not touch the large Jars (PYTHOI) which are left in their natural positions, do not walk over mosaics. In general, do look after them.

No excavations of any kind are allowed without permission and the removal of items is strictly prohibited, as it is to export any kind of antiquities.

PUBLIC HOLIDAYS

The following are public holidays which are observed in Crete:

- JANAURY 1 — New Year's Day
- JANUARY 6 — Epiphany
- CLEAN MONDAY (Kathari Deftera) — First Monday after Lent — Movable
- GOOD FRIDAY & EASTER SUNDAY/ MONDAY—Orthodox Easter — Movable
- MARCH 25 — Greek Independence Day
- ASCENSION DAY — Movable
- MAY 1 — May Day and Spring Festival
- AUGUST 15 — Assumption of Virgin Mary
- OCTOBER 28 — OXI (NO-DAY)
- NOVEMBER 7 — ARKADI DAY
- DECEMBER 25 & 26 — Christmas & Boxing Day

FESTIVALS—EVENTS

Crete provides many colourful festivals, some are religious, some celebrating national events and others celebrating various products of Crete.

NEW YEAR — A welcome to the new year at midnight, sharing out a cake with a coin hidden and continue celebrating up to the early hours. During the day, feasting and other celebrations continue. One custom is to open the windows to let the evil spirits out.

EPIPHANY-JAN. 6 – Ceremonies take place at seaside resorts when a blessed cross is thrown into the water and young divers compete to recover it. Various games take place.

CARNIVAL — One of the most colourful festivals in Crete. It starts in late February or early March (movable), 2 weeks before lent and reaches its climax at the last weekend with parades in the streets, dancing, singing romantic songs and eating. Biggest celebrations take place at Rethymno and Heraklion.

CLEAN MONDAY (Kathari Deftera) – The first Monday of Lent. After the excessiveness of the Carnival, the body is cleaned by eating only vegetables. It is customary for families to go to the countryside for picnics and kites are flying everywhere.

EASTER — Greek Orthodox Easter is more important (in celebrations) than Christmas. The Easter week services depict the last days of Jesus' life. His arrest on Thursday and His Crucifixion on Friday and His Burial in a bier covered with all sorts of flowers. Saturday midnight is the Resurrection "CHRISTOS ANESTI (Jesus is Risen) with candle light processions and the breaking of dyed eggs. Sunday is a day of happiness and family celebrations with the traditional roasting of lamb.

MARCH 25 — Greek Independence day in commemoration of the Popular Uprising of 25 March 1821 against the Turkish Occupation. Parades take place followed by athletic events, dances and firework displays.

ST. THOMAS DAY — 1st Sunday after Easter. Religious celebrations take place at the monas-

Apart from the planned events, any festival activity is an invitation for everyone to participate.

tery of VRONTISI *(Heraklion district)* and NEO KHORIO of Apokorona *(Hania district).*

ORANGE FESTIVAL — April. Takes place at SKINES KYDONIAS *(Hania)*, with exhibitions, Cretan folk music and dancing.

ST. GEORGE'S DAY — Movable in the spring. A popular event in Crete and most important celebrations take place at the monastery of EPANOSIFI *(Heraklion)* where the Archbishop celebrates mass.

ASCENSION DAY — At ALMYROS church near Ayios Nikolaos *(Lasithi)*. A religious event celebrated in many places with fireworks, feasts, music and dancing.

MAY 1st — Parades; picnics; dancing; a flower wreath is placed over the front door of each house to celebrate the coming of spring.

MAY 20-27 — A week starting around the 20th to celebrate the BATTLE OF CRETE in 1941. Celebrations with athletic events and exhibitions take place.

At Khora Sfakion they celebrate their anniversary of the 1821 Revolution.

JUNE 24 — St. John the Baptist's Birthday. Also SUMMER SOLSTICE with bonfires lit and the wreaths of flowers from May 1st are burned.

Important is the KLIDONA FESTIVAL at Kroustas *(Lasithi)* with Cretan folklore.

JULY-MARINE WEEK — First week of the month, with sea sports in many coastal towns.

JULY 17 — Hersonissos WATER MELON Festival. Also at Voni Village (Heraklion), a major religious festival of St. Marina.

JULY-WINE FESTIVAL — Around the middle of the month. A festival takes place at Dafnes village (Heraklion). Most important is at RETHYMNO *(end of July)* with free wine sampling, dancing, eating and Cretan folklore.

AUGUST — SULTANA GRAPE FESTIVAL at Sitia. A continuous celebration taking about 5 days.

AUGUST 15 — ASSUMPTION of OUR Lady — Virgin Mary. This is a big religious festival throughout the Greek World. In Crete most important locations at NEAPOLIS *(Lasithi)* with sports and dances and at MOKHLOS village *(Heraklion)* organised by the Greek Touring Club with fireworks, food, drinking and dancing.

AUGUST — KRITSA Village *(Lasithi)*. Old customs and traditions festival with a mock wedding of Cretan style. Check for date from Tourist Information Office.

OCTOBER — CHESTNUT festival in many villages of the Hania district. Cretan folklore during the month.

OCTOBER 28 — OHI DAY *(NO-DAY)* Commemorating the Greek Negative answer to the Italian forces demand to march into Greece from Albania in 1940.

NOVEMBER 7-9 — ARKADI celebrations commemorating the resistance of the Cretan enclaves in the monastery against the Turks and the explosion which occurred; they chose to die rather surrender.

DECEMBER 25th — CHRISTMAS DAY

Please Note: Some events may be cancelled, others change dates and new ones may be introduced. For an up-to-date programme, please consult the Greek Tourist Information Office of the district of your stay in Crete.

The traditional ornamental **Bread** of Marriage

SPORTS
SEA SPORTS

SWIMMING — This is the most common and popular activity of tourists whether by the sea or the swimming pool, do take care of the sun; it is always hotter than it seems and if you expose yourself too much, you will end up with painful burns and unhappy holidays.

There are countless beaches, some popular, others isolated. Organised swimming beaches in all main tourist places provide facilities and tavernas. These are to be found by most other beaches offering drinks, snacks even meals. When swimming, be wary of deep waters which can be hazardous to less able swimmers. In some areas currents or undercurrents can be dangerous, for everyone, so look for the notices.

In some remote places you can sunbathe in the nude although nudism is not allowed in Crete and you must respect the feelings of local people. However, topless bathing and sunbathing is well established and accepted everywhere.

BOATING/SAILING — The numerous ports and small fishing harbours can supply small boats for hire for short or long excursions. Protected bays are safer but otherwise be careful for unexpected and sudden winds, which can become hazardous to inexperienced people.

Water skiing, wind surfing, boating are provided by many hotels and other centres and in some places sailing boats can be hired.

At Hania the Maritime Club Tel. 24387 can assist.

SKIN-DIVING — Scuba diving is not widely organised and generally not allowed to those without special permits except for those who are members of organised and permitted clubs.

Snorkelling is very popular and the offshore sea bed provides much that is beautiful plus the occasional submerged ruin. One of the most interesting places is that of Mirabello Bay.

FISHING — No licence is required for anglers to enjoy fishing by the coast. Hiring a boat for deep water fishing can be arranged in most seaside centres although fish around Crete is not plentiful. There can be restrictions on fishing with a fishing gun or spear so consult the tourist police or harbour master if you wish to use one.

OTHER SPORTS

TENNIS — There are two tennis Clubs:
Heraklion Tennis Club: Beaufort Avenue Tel. 283015
Hania Tennis Club: Dimokratias Avenue Tel. 21293/4
All are welcome and lessons can be arranged.

HIKING/CLIMBING/POT HOLING — Crete provides fascinating mountains to be explored and the views of the lands below are magnificent. Caves of many types and sizes provide excitement. Excursions can be very rewarding and there are clubs in both Heraklion and Hania organising professional group excursions.

SKIING — Snow falls in the high peaks and provide ideal conditions for skiers. The Greek Alpine Club has established mountain refuges at:
LEFKAORI KALERGI—Altitude 1600m, ski lift, 40 bunks — Tel. Hania 24647
LEFKAORI VOLIKAS-Altitude 1480m, 30 bunks — Tel. Hania 24647
PSILORITIS PRINOS—Altitude 1100m 16 bunks — Tel. Heraklion 287110

Relaxing by the beach — Matala.

HORSE TREKKING — The best organised is near Heraklion and information can be obtained from the Tourist Information Office.

HUNTING — This is a popular Cretan sport but is only allowed in certain areas and at strictly observed seasons. Hares, rabbits, birds are the victims of this sport.

Above: "OFI" the top Cretan Football team and one of the best in Greece is based in Heraklion

Below: Ayia Pelaghia—Kapsis beach with its ideal boating facilities. This can be found in most other Cretan holiday resorts.

SHOPPING

During the summer, shops open around 8am-8pm with a break *(siesta)* from 1.30-4.30pm. During winter they open later, close earlier and have much shorter lunch breaks. Early closing is usually Wednesday and Saturday and remain closed on Sunday. In tourist areas shops have more flexible hours. Government regulations may soon alter the above opening/closing times.

KIOSKS — boxed shops to be found on wide pavements or by the street corners and squares open most of the time and sell basic items such as sweets, chocolates, tobacco, films, toilet articles, pens, souvenirs, magazines, newspapers, even stamps with an added charge for service.

OPEN MARKETS to be found in all towns are a delight to visit. Explore the food stalls, the souvenirs and even clothes, leather goods etc.

Crete offers a big variety of items and prices vary from place to place. In some places you may use the art of bargaining although many shops now indicate their prices which are fixed.

FINE FABRICS — include clothing, bedspreads, pillow cases, tagaria *(shoulder bags)*.

HAND KNITTED — knitwear, carpets, lace, embroidery, textiles.

LEATHERWORK — coats, boats *(almost an art in Crete)*, handbags.

JEWELLERY — Excellent gold and silver jewellery is expensive but well worth the money as it is of excellent design and quality. Some exquisite designs are based on Minoan styles.

SOUVENIRS — include reproductions of Minoan art, vases, knives, worry beads, icons, wood carvings, ceramics.

FOODSTUFFS – including nuts, excellent coffee, sweets.

TRADITIONAL HANDICRAFT — The National Organisation of Greek Handicrafts provides two main showrooms where visitors can see items in permanent display rooms.
HERAKLION: Zographou & Chourdou St. Tel. (081) 280225
HANIA: 6 Tombazi Street. Tel. (0821) 22568.

Above: A souvenir shop. Below: Woven item with Cretan motifs.

Cretan Leather Goods and the famous Cretan knives are very popular.

TRAVELLING IN CRETE

Ancient Cretan Roads can be traced in some places. The Minoans had an extremely good road system. The Venetians established good roads with paved stones and some were very busy with traffic.

But the roads deteriorated and were almost completely destroyed under the Turkish occupation. From that time onwards the only way to travel was by mule or horse for the rich or by donkey for the poor.

It was in the 1910's when a serious effort was made to build roads and the main Hania to Heraklion connection started. It was completed in 1936. The road network was badly damaged during the war of 1939-45 and further deterioration continued for a short while after the war.

In 1965 the Cretan Development Plan was established and a massive road building scheme commenced thus giving a new lease of life to both agriculture and tourism. As a result, Crete has now an excellent road system and an enlarged and well organised bus system.

Driving is on the right hand side of the road as it is in all other countries of Europe except the United Kingdom, Ireland, Malta and Cyprus.

HIRING A CAR — This is easy, in all tourist areas there are many Car-Hire firms, some of International stature and some well organised local firms. However, during the busy summer months the demand increases and it is wise to book through your travel agent.

The rates are officially regulated and most firms offer similar rates. Shop around for bargains by checking how they charge you, daily? weekly? and with limited or unlimited mileage? It's also wise to check carefully the type of insurance offered.

MOTOR BIKES — These are plentiful in most tourist areas and are an ideal way of travelling short distances. But do take great care when riding, as accidents can often end your holiday in total misery.

TAXIS — An ideal way to travel around in the major towns. Do not be surprised if other passengers are picked up on the way to share the taxi; this is customary throughout Greece. Taxis also have connections with many villages. If you set up for long journeys by taxi, it is advisable to negotiate the charges so that you can avoid surprises at the other end.

COACHES — Several tourist agencies arrange coach excursions; some have regular excursions to the main places of interest and in many cases there are officially appointed guides.

BUSES — There are excellent bus connections with all towns and major villages and some archaeological sites. More details are given under each of the four districts.

During the summer months, some services are increased to meet the extra demand.

151

BY SEA — Some sea connections from harbour to harbour are done with the KAÏKI — a type of local fisherman's boat. Some are local services and others can be arranged by special payments. *YACHTING* is an ideal way to get around the island. Adequate facilities exist at Heraklion, Hania, Rethymno, Sitia and Ierapetra. But remember, the sea on the northern side of Crete can be rough at times.

Should you require further information about Yachting, please contact the Greek National Tourist Organisation, Yachting Department: 4 Stadiou Street, Athens or the Heraklion Yacht Club by the Venetian Castle.

TRAVELLING DISTANCES IN KMS

	HERAKLION	HANIA	RETHYMNO	IERAPETRA	AYIOS NICOLAOS	HERSO-NISSOS	SITIA	KASTELLI	OMALOS	AYIA GALINI	MALIA	ANOYIA	KRITSA
KRITSA	86	228	158	42	6	60	78	270	267	158	49	114	—
ANOYIA	28	124	54	144	108	54	180	166	163	100	65	—	114
MALIA	37	179	129	79	43	11	115	221	218	109	—	65	49
AYIA GALINI	72	126	56	188	152	98	224	168	165	—	109	100	158
OMALOS	181	39	109	297	261	207	333	81	—	165	218	163	267
KASTELLI	184	42	112	300	264	210	336	—	81	168	221	166	270
SITIA	152	294	224	118	72	126	—	336	333	224	115	180	78
HERSONISSOS	26	168	98	90	54	—	126	210	207	98	11	54	60
AYIOS NICOLAOS	80	222	152	36	—	54	72	264	261	152	43	108	6
IERAPETRA	116	258	188	—	36	90	118	300	297	188	79	144	42
RETHYMNO	72	70	—	188	152	98	224	112	109	56	129	54	158
HANIA	142	—	70	258	222	168	294	42	39	126	179	124	228
HERAKLION	—	142	72	116	80	26	152	184	181	72	37	28	86

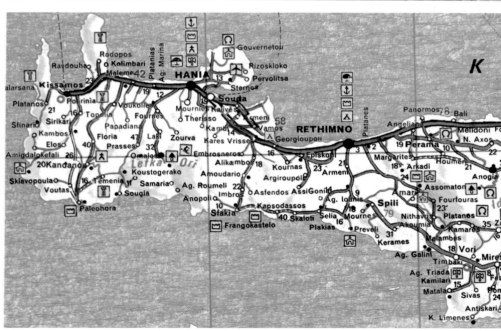

ENTERTAINMENT

The Cretans are masters at enjoying themselves. Any visitor who shares their natural love for the enjoyment of life is most welcome to participate.

MUSIC-BOUZOUKI CLUBS — To be found mainly in Heraklion and Hania, more in the open air during the summer. They provide first class entertainment. They start around 11pm and continue up to 3 or 4am. They usually sell drinks in bottles, whisky being the most popular, but mezedhes can be seved, although it is customary for the locals to go previously to a local taverna.

The Bouzouki music is loud with hypnotic rhythms. Every band has a leading Bouzouki musician. Singers both male or female, solo or in groups, sing all the popular Greek songs and the people join in mainly dancing to the music with movements expressing their own individual interpretation of the sound.

Others offer flowers or champagne to the singer of their liking to show their appreciation and others will break plates *(special ones)* to release their sheer happiness.

CRETAN CLUBS — These provide mainly Cretan music and dancing and the atmosphere can be exhilarating. *LYRA* is the main musical instrument, a variation of a violin rested on the knees. The sound of the music is sharp and exotic and the dancing movements very powerful.

Cretan dancing movements include:
CHANIOTIKOS — originated from Hania and dancers form a circle
PENDOZALI — dancers interlock their arms
SYRTOS — a circle dance
Lyra music and Cretan dancing in traditional costumes are performed at numerous festivals and special events staged for the tourists.

DISCO MUSIC — All tourist centres have numerous discotheques some of excellent quality and atmosphere and can be certain that all the latest European chart hits are played. Drinks are served in the discotheques and in some places an entrance fee is charged.

EATING OUT

The Cretans, not only are masters in enjoying music and dancing but also masters in eating. Therefore, their food is of high standards in quality and taste.

For those wishing to experience Cretan food and atmosphere as the locals do, should search for the tavernas frequented by Cretans.

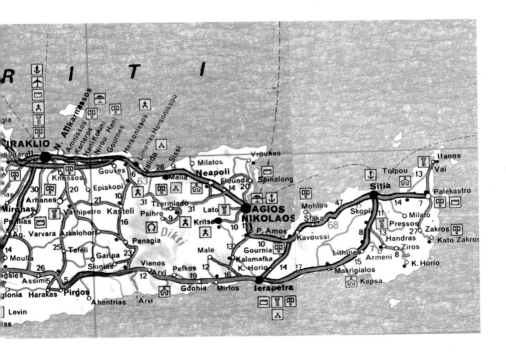

Other tavernas or restaurants are excellent but cater more for European tastes.

THE TAVERNAS will either provide general Greek food or Cretan specialities or you can try their special meze food which is a selection of various specialities.

THE FISH TAVERNAS by the coastal resorts provide delicious fresh fish, expensive for Crete, but much less than most other European countries.

In most tavernas you can inspect the fish or look at the selection of cooked meals before deciding what to eat.

RESTAURANTS. These are more formal than tavernas and conform to western type of food. and some are more expensive.

EXOHIKO KENTRO is a rural centre, a mixture of cafe and taverna.

PATISSERIE (Zaharoplastio). These are common in squares where they occupy large spaces, they serve refreshments, coffee, cakes and pastries.

KAFENION. To be found in every corner of towns and villages, the Cretan equivalent of a pub, where the locals, mainly the men, gather for a chat, for a drink of OUZO or RAKI or sip their coffee (indicate according to preference) — GLYKO (sweet with lots of sugar), METRIO (medium with a bit of sugar) or SKETTO (without sugar).

The locals spend their time reading newspapers, talking politics and trying to solve all the world's problems or playing cards and tavli (backgammon).

CRETAN DISHES

Below we mention some of the most popular Cretan Dishes which are common to most other Greek places.

HORS D'OEUVRE (OPECTICA)
- TARAMOSALATA — Dip of fish roe paste
- DOLMADHES YALANTZI — Stuffed vine leaves with egg, lemon sauce, served hot.
- TZAZIKI — Yoghurt, garlic and cucumber dip

SOUPS (SOUPES)
- AVGOLEMONO — Rice and egg — lemon sauce soup
- HORTOSOUPA — Vegetable soup
- MAGHERITSA — An Easter speciality — a tripe soup with rice
- PSAROSOUPA — Fish soup with vegetables and lemon sauce.

PASTA-RICE (ZEMARIKA)
- PILAFI — Pilaf rice with sauce
- SPAGHETTO-MAKARONI — Spaghetti with sauce and cheese
- PASTICHIO — Makaroni with mince, herbs and cheese sauce
- RAVIOLI — the local type is a delight and is very popular.

FISH (PSARIA)
- BARBOUNI — Red Mullet
- SINAGRIDHA — Red Snapper
- LITHRINIA — Bass
- MARIDHES — White Bait
- KALAMARI — Squid

A Modern Discotheque at Hersonissos.

154

Fresh fish is expensive but when found is extraordinary and deliciously cooked.

- GARIDHES — Prawns
- OCTABODY — Octopus
- ASTAKOS — Lobster
- STRIDHIA — Oysters

ENTREES (ENTRADES)
- ARNAKI FASOLAKI — Lamb with green beans in tomato sauce. Other vegetables are also served this way.
- MOSKHARI PSIDO — Roast Veal
- KOTOPOULO PSIDO — Roast Chicken
- KHINA PSIDO — Roast Goose
- GEMISTA — Stuffed with rice and mince meat, aubergines, tomatoes or peppers
- MOUSAKA — Layers of aubergines, potatoes, tomatoes, minced beef and cheese sauce
- TSOUTSOUKAKIA — Meat balls in tomato sauce
- KOTOLETTES KHIRINES — Pork Cutlets
- STIFADO — Beef stew with herbs and onions
- KOKORETSI — Lamb's liver, kidney, sweetbreads and heart wrapped in intestines.

GRILLS (TIS SKARAS)
- SOUVLAKIA — Kebabs pork or lamb, cooked over charcoal
- KOTOPOULLO — Grilled chicken
- BRIZOLES MOSKHARISHES — Veal chops
- KEFTEDHES SKARAS — Grilled meat balls
- GOUROUNOPOULLO — Suckling Pig
- PAIDAKIA KHIRINIA — Pork chops

SALADS (SALADES)
- TOMATOSALATA — Tomatoes, olives, onions, fetta
- KHORIATIKI — Lettuce, tomatoes, olives, onions, peppers, cucumber, fetta
  - PIPERIES — Greek peppers, tomatoes
  - ROUSSIKI — Russian salad
  - VRASTA — Boiled vegetables with lemon and oil sauce including courgettes, artichokes etc.

CHEESE (TYRIA)
- FETTA — White soft goats milk cheese
- GRAVIERA and KEFALOGRAVIERA — The special Cretan Cheese
- KASSERI — Hard yellow cheese

PASTRY PIES (PITTA)
- TYROPITTA — Small pies with cheese
- SPANAKOPITTA — delicious pies filled spinach

MEZEDHES — This a selection of many of the above items over 6 and in some places up to 16 different items brought on to your table at intervals. An ideal way to taste most of the Greek Specialities, suitable for two or larger groups.

SWEETS (GLYGA)
- BOUGATSA — A Cretan speciality brought in by Armenians. A delicate pastry filled either with cheese or custard and sprinkled with sugar (optional)
- LOUKOUMADHES — Plain dough balls, deep fried and served in sesame seed and honey sauce
- BAKLAVA — Nuts and honey pastry
- KATAIFI — Wheat and honey pastry
- RIZOGALO — Rice pudding
- YIAOURTI — Yoghurt. A speciality in some places eaten on its own or with honey or cheese.

CRETAN WINES
No meal can be enjoyed without the delicious taste of a good Greek wine and Crete produces some of the best in the country. They come from ancient **Vineyards** as old as the Minoans, the backbone of the Cretan economy and rural life. Slope after slope and valley after valley is covered with well-looked after vineyards.

Wines Include:
Red Brands. **Brouskos** and **Kissamos**
White Brands: **Minos, Gortinos, Phestos**
The best sweet dessert is **Malevizi**.

RAKI is a very strong Cretan drink-spirit and comes from the pips of grapes. Any kafenion should have some to offer instead of coffee. But be warned, it is strong.

WELCOME TO CRETE
USEFUL GREEK WORDS and PHRASES

Cretans are well known for their hospitality and friendliness and it is this traditic that we want to preserve and enhance with our publication.

Having in mind that most of those who are going to use our Travel Guide may n know the alphabet, we have transliterated all the Greek words in Roman characte to help them with the pronunciation.

Key to Pronunciation:

a is pronounced as in fat	i as in hit	p as in balance
dh as th in three	o as in not	ss as s in see
e as in ten	ou as u in put	th as in thick
gh as y in yet		

GREETINGS-HERETISMI

good morning......kaliméra
good evening.......kalispéra
good night........kalinihta
hello..............yiá
good bye..........adio
glad to meet you ...hárika yia ti ghnorimia

NUMBERS-ARITHMI

one ....éna	eleven ....éndeka
two ....dhio	twelve ....dhódheka
three...tria	thirteen........dhekatria
four ...téssera	fourteen ....dhekatéssera
five ....pénde	for others ......dhekapénda etc.
six .....éxi	twenty ....ikossi
seven ..eptá	twenty one etc ..ikossiéna etc.
eight...októ	thirty ....triandha
nine ...ennéa	one hundred ....ekató
ten.....dhéka	one thousnd ....hilia
	one million......éna ekatomirio

DRIVING A CAR – ME TO AFTOKINITO

where can I hire a car? ....poú boró na enikiasso ena aftokinito?
how much is it by day? ....pósso káni tin iméra?
how much is petrol?...........pósso káni i ventzini?
how far is a petrol station?......pósso makriá ine énas stathmos ventzinis?
where can I find a mechanic? ...pou boró an vró ena mihanikó?
check the oil and water please ..parakaló dhéste to ládi ke to neró
something is wrong with my car — kati éhi to aftokinito mou
where does this road lead to? ...pou pái aftós o dhrómos?

SIGHTSEEING – STA AXIOTHÉATA

is there a sightseeing tour round the city................ipáchi ekdhromi sta axiothéata tis polis?
what time does the coach leave? póte févgi to leoforio?
how much time will the tour take? ....póssi óra tha dhiarkessi i periodhia?
what is the fare?...............póssa ine to issitirio?
we want to see the Archaeological museum ....théloume na dhoúme to Archeologhikó moussio
is the museum of Folk Art open on Sundays?.............ine to moussio laikistehnis anihtó tis Kyriakés
how much is the entrance fee? póssa ine i issodhos?
where can I get a catalogue? ....poú boró na páro ena katálogo?
is there an Art Gallery? ....iparhi pinakothiki?
can we take pictures?...........boroúme na vgháloume fotographies?

ON THE BEACH – STIN BARALÍA (PLÁZ)

where can we go swimming? ...poú boroúme na páme yia kolimbi?
can you suggest a good beach? borite na issighithite mia kali pláz?
how far is it?.................pósso makria ine?
how can I get there?...........pos boró na páo eki?
I would like to hire an umbrella thá ithela na enikiasso miá ombrélla
I need a suntan oil ....thélo ládhi yia ton ilio
I want something for sunburn thélo káti yia kápsimo apo ton ilio
can you give me a small first aid kit? ....borite na mou dhósete ena mikró kouti próton voithión?
I want something for insect bites ....thélo káti yia tsimbimata entómon

POLICE - ASTINOMIA

I had an accident............iha éna atihima
can you call the police?.......borite na kaléssete tin
astinomia? (asfália)
where is the police station? .... poú ine o astinomikós
stathmós?
where is the British embassy? . poú ine i Angliki presvia?
I have lost my traveller's
cheques ··············· éhasa ta traveller's cheques

AT THE BANK - STIN TRÁPEZA

I want to change some money thélo na alláxo hrimata
what is the rate of exhange? ...pia ine i timi synallágmatos?
can you give me some small
change?...................... mou dhinete meriká psilá?
do you change traveller's   Allazete
cheques?.............. travellers cheques?
cashier..................... .tamias
coin........................ .nómisma
bank note .... hartonómisma

POST - TAHIDROMIO

I want to send a letter........thélo na stilo éna ghrámma
is there a post office nearby? ..ipárhi tahidromio kondá?
where can I find a post box? ...pou boró na vró grammato-
kivotio?
I want to send this letter   thélo na stilo aftó to
express ············ ···· grámma epighon
I want to send this letter ..... thélo na stilo aftó to
registered .... grámma sistiméno
I need some stamps .... thélo meriká ghrammatosima

AT THE DOCTOR - STO YIATRÓ

I am ill...................... ime árostos
I have a fever .... ého piretó
I have a headache .... ého ponokéfalo
I have a cold................ ého kriológima
can you call a doctor? .... borite na fonáxete éna yiatró?
take me to the hospital, please.. párte me sto nossokomio,
parakaló

SHOPPING - PSÓNIA

buy	aghorázo	choose	dhialégho	ice cream	paghotó	toothpaste	odhondó-krema
sell	pouló	colour	khróma	drinks	potá	rope	skini
sale	xepoúlima	chicken	kotópoullo	discount	ékptossi	shoe lace	kordhóni papoutsión
cheap	ftinó	lamb	arni	clothes	roúha		
expensive	akrivó	beef	vodhinó	bathing costume mayió		camera	photogra-phiki mihani
give	dhino	pork	hirinó	size	méghethos		
owe	hrostó	potato	patáta	brush	vourtsa	envelope	fákelos
price	timí	fruit	froúto	toothbrush	odhondó-vourtsa	perfume	ároma
quality	piotita	fish	psári			petrol	venzini
change (to)	al-lázo						

where is the market? ....poú ine i aghorá?
when do the shops close? .....póte klioun tá katastimata?
I just want to look around ....thélo na rixo mia matiá
could you show me?..........borite na mou dhixete?
I like that one in the window.. thélo aftó sti vitrina?
can I try it on................boró na to dhokimasso?
how much is this...........póso stihizi?/póso kostizi?
have you anything cheaper? ...éhete tipote ftinótero?
I need a pair of shoes........thélo éna zevghari papoútsia
I want to fill my lighter   thélo na ghemisso ton
with gas ....anaptira mou me gázi
where can I buy English   poú boró na aghoráss
newspapers?   Anglikés efimeridhes?
I want some postcards .... thélo merikes kártes
(karts-posta)

can I listen to the record?........boró na akoússo to dhisko?
I need a 35mm film with 20   thélo éna film ton triantapéde
with 36 exposures ....ghia fotographies triandhaéxi
do you have a cartridge for this éhete kassétta ghia afti ti
camera?......................fotographiki mihani?
do you have a battery for this? éhete bataria ghia afti?
I would like some souvenirs ....thélo na dhó meriká idhi
hirotehnias
I would like to buy a doll in   tha ithela no aghoráso mia
local dress ....koúkla me topiki endhimassia
I would like to see some needle tha ithela no dhó meriká
embroidery ....kentimata me smili
I want to buy a woven napkin ...thélo na agorásso mia ifandi
petsétta
have you got any pieces of .....éhete kathólou assimiká?
silver work?

BASIC PHRASES

yes	ne	I want	thelo	it is expensive	ine akrivó
no	óhi	do you understand		what is this?	ti ine aftó?
thank you	efharistó	me?	me katalavénete?	sometimes	kápote
who?	piós?	speak more slowly,	miláte pió argha,	I am afraid	fovoúme
where?	poú?	please	parakaló	I am tired	ime kourasménos
when?	póte?	what do you say?	ti léte?	its early	ine enoris
why?	yiati?	with pleasure	efharistos	it's late	ine arghá
how?	pós?	I agree	symfonó	ask (to)	rotó
how are you?	pós iste?	you are right	éhete dhikeo	answer (to)	apandó
very well	poli kalá	you are wrong	éhete ádhiko	apologise (to)	zitó sighnómi
excuse me	signomi	everything right?	óla endáxi?	today	simera
what is your name	pos onomazesse?	I am ready	ime étimos	now	tora
	or pos se léne	I am in a hurry	viázome	immediately	améssos
can you help me	borite na me	I know that	to xéro aftó		
	voithisete?	it is nice	ine oréo		

where is the market?	poú ine i aghorá?	can I listen to the record?	boróan akoússo to dhisko?
when do the shops close?	póte klioun tá katastimata?	I need a 35mm film with 20	thélo éna film ton triantapéde
I just want to look around	thélo na rixo mia matiá	with 36 exposures	ghia fotographies triandhaéxi
could you show me?	borite na mou dhixete?	do you have a cartridge for this	éhete kassétta ghia afti ti
I like that one in the window	thélo aftó sti vitrina?	camera?	fotographiki mihani?
can I try it on	boró na to dhokimasso?	do you have a battery for this?	éhete bataria ghia afti?
how much is this	póso stihizi?/póso kostizi?	I would like some souvenirs	thélo na dhó meriká idhi
have you anything cheaper?	éhete tipote ftinótero?		hirotehnias
I need a pair of shoes	thélo éna zevghari	I would like to buy a doll in	tha ithela no aghoráso mia
	papoútsia	local dress	koúkla me topiki endhimassia
I want to fill my lighter	thélo na ghemisso ton	I would like to see some needle	tha ithela no dhó meriká
with gas	anaptira mou me gázi	embroidery	kentimata me smili
where can I buy English	poú boró na aghoráss	I want to buy a woven napkin	thélo na agorásso mia ifandi
newspapers?	Anglikés efimeridhes?		petsétta
I want some postcards	thélo merikes kártes	have you got any pieces of	éhete kathólou assimiká?
	(karts-posta)	silver work?	

RESTAURANT - ESTIADÓRION

bread	psomi	I am hungry	pinó	can you recommend a good	borite na mou sistissete
butter	voútiro	knife	mahéri	restaurant?	ena kaló estiatório?
cheese	tiri	meat	kréas	I would like a table for two	éna trapézi giá dhio parakaló
dessert	ghlikó	milk	ghala	I didn't make a reservation	dhen krátissa trapézi
egg	avghó	refreshments	anapsiktiká	I would prefer a table by the	protimó éna trapezi kondá
fork	pirouni	salad	saláta	window	stó parathiro
fruit	froúto	salt	aláti	May I see the menu, please?	boró na dhó to menu
glass	potiri	sausage	loukániko		parakalo?
sea food	psariká	I am thirsty	dhipsó	What do you recommend?	ti sistinete?
serve	serviro	tip	filodhórima	What are the specialities of	pia ine ta specialité tou
soup	soúpa	tomato	tomáta	your restaurant?	estiatoriou sas?
spoon	koutáli	waiter	servitoros	a bottle of wine, please	parakaló mia boukála krassi
sugar	záhari	waitress	servitóra	glass of bear, please	éna potiri bira, parakaló
taste	ghéfsi	water	neró	may I have a bottle of mineral	boro naého mia boukála
tea	tsai	ashtray	stahtodhohio	water?	metallikó neró?
				I would like another glass of	tha ithela akomi ena potiri
				water	neró
				a cup of tea, please	parakaló éna flitzani tsái

158

one medium coffee and one...	éna metrio ke éna ghlikó	do you take traveller's cheques?	dhéheste traveller's cheques?
sweet	kafé	Will you take English currency?	pérnete Anglika hrimata?
the bill please	to loghariasmó parakaló	Will you take foreign currency?	pérnete xéna hrimata?
we would like separate bills ...	tha thélame xehoristoús logariasmoús		

HOTEL - XENOTHOHIO

bell	koudhoúni	I want a single room with a	thélo éna monó dhomátio me
chambermaid ..	kamariera	shower?	doúch
dining room	trapezaria	I want a room with a double bed	thélo éna dhomátio me dipló
discotheque	dhiskothiki		kreváti
electric point ...	priza	and a bathoom	ke bánio
elevator	assansér	I would like a room with sea view	tha ithela éna dhomátio me
lavatory	apohoritirio		théa sti thálassa
mosquito	kounoupi	is the room air-conditioned?.....	to dhomatio éhi air condition?
pillow	maxilari	is there a television in the room?	to dhomátio éhi tileórassi?
press	sidheróno	is there a telephone in the room?	to dhomátio éhi tiléfono?
sanatary	petsétes	what floor is the room on?......	se pión órofon ine to
towels	ighias		dhomátio?
soap	sapouni	may I see the room?	boró na dhó to dhomátio?
stay	méno	can I leave this in your safe?...	boró na to afisso aftó sto
swimming pool	pissina		hrimatokivótio sas?
toilet paper....	hartí toualéttas	what time is breakfast served?	ti ora ine to próghevma?
key	klidhí	what time is lunch?	ti óra ine to messimeriano?
room..........	dhomátio	are there any messages for me?	ého kanena minima?
reception	ipodhohi	I would like the bill	thá ithela to loghariasmó
		It is a nice room..............	ine kaló to dhomátio
		can I have breakfast in my	boró naého to próghevma
		room please?	stó dhomátio mou, parakaló?
		can I have some more hangers?	boró náého akómi ligha
name is....................	to ónoma mou/légome		kremastária?
ve you got a room for the	éhete éna dhomátio yia	I can't find any towels in my	dhen éhi petsétes sto
ht?........................	apópse?	room........................	dhomátio mou
w much is the room per night?	pósso káni to dhomatio yia ti	may I have another blanket?....	boró aného akómi miá
	nihta?		kouvérta?
w much is the room without	pósso káni to dhomátio horis	may I have another pillow?	boró náého akómi ena
als?	fayitá?		maxilári?

CRETAN CIVIL LIFE

It was around 450BC when the Civil Laws and Life in general were written on many tablets found at Gortys. Not much has changed since then in human behaviour although the modern needs of society has changed in ages.

THE CHURCH — All Greeks are Orthodox Christians although in Crete there is a small community of Catholics and other denominations.

CIVIL ADMINISTRATION — Crete has 4 large administrative DISTRICTS called "NOMOI" which has been described in detail in earlier pages.

Each nomos has **Eparhia** (*Rural districts*): The town authorities are called **Dimos** and the rural communes are called **Kinotis**.

The central government of Athens has regional offices based in Heraklion including a Ministry of Co-ordination (*development and planning*). Ministry of Agriculture Department of Trade and Industry and Department of Mercantile Marine.

LAW-COURTS — Minor offences are tried by summary courts in towns, presided over by a local magistrate. Serious crimes and civil cases of importance are presided over by a higher court. There are appeal courts and the highest is the Supreme Court in Athens.

Public Order is administered by the Police (*KHOROPHYLAKI*). Their functions cover towns, villages and the countryside. There is a branch dealing with all traffic aspects and is called *TROHEA*.

The New Cretans although strong in their traditions they dress and look like other Europeans. But the old with their traditional way of dressing and appearance may be a thing of the past. We salute their resolute way of life and wish them many years of active life.

THE CRETANS

As a final section we would like to pay homage to all Cretans, some of the proudest and most hospitable people in the Mediterranean.

They will greet a stranger out of respect, they may even want to shake hands, a natural Cretan way of saying "Hello". In shops or markets, away from tourist places, a visitor may be asked to sample some food before purchasing or be offered coffee or a drink. This is a form of appreciation. During the Siesta, a Cretan "must not" be disturbed. It is important to rest and be relaxed.

Do not double cross a Cretan, because he will not forgive you. But you help or assist one and he will remember you forever. It is a Cretan's pleasure to assist someone in need. In company of locals, do not be shy to ask personal questions; this is customary and part of daily Greek conversation.

If you are invited out for a meal, do not attempt to pay or share the bill. This will be taken as an insult. If you feel strongly, then repay their kindness with something else.

Do not drink slowly and leave your glass half empty. In Crete do not feel shy to take your children everywhere you go at night. They love their children and they take them to the taverna. It is part of their growing up to participate with their family.